9/01

WRITING FROM THE HEART

Watch your thoughts, they become words

Watch your words, they become actions

Watch your actions, they become habits

Watch your habits, they become your character

Watch your character, it becomes your destiny.

—Anonymous

WRITING *from the* HEART

YOUNG PEOPLE SHARE THEIR WISDOM

Edited by Peggy Veljkovic and Arthur J. Schwartz, Ed.D.

Foreword by Sir John Templeton

Best of the Laws of Life *Essay Contest*

TEMPLETON FOUNDATION PRESS • PHILADELPHIA & LONDON

TEMPLETON FOUNDATION PRESS
Five Radnor Corporate Center, Suite 120
100 Matsonford Road
Radnor, Pennsylvania 19087

Library of Congress Cataloging-in-Publication Data

Writing from the heart : Young people share their wisdom / edited by
Peggy Veljkovic and Arthur J. Schwartz
    p. cm. (Best of the laws of life essay contest)
  Includes index.
  ISBN: 1-890151-48-3 (pbk. : alk. paper)
   1. Youth—Conduct of life. I. Veljkovic, Peggy, 1967–
  II. Schwartz, Arthur J., 1954–
BJ21661 .I2 2000
170—dc21   00-064818

For more information about the *Laws of Life* Essay Contest,
contact the John Templeton Foundation at 800-245-1285
(U.S. only) or 610-687-8942 or visit our website at
www.lawsoflife.org.

To order call 800-621-2736 OR 773-568-1550

Executive Editor: Patricia Roarty
Contributing Editors: Sharon Sizgorich, Therese Boyd, and Jack Roarty
Designer & Typesetter: Gopa and the Bear
Printer: R.R. Donnelley & Sons Company
Printed in the United States of America

Special thanks to Pamela Thompson, Lynn Glodek, and Vlada Veljkovic,
who have generously contributed their time and talents to this publication.

All proceeds from the sale of *Writing from the Heart* will help fund the
printing of future volumes.

Cover photographs © SuperStock, Inc. and Photodisc
Photo on page 8 courtesy of Harper Run Communication Arts/Bob Conway
Photo on page 56 courtesy of David Fahleson

01 02 03 04 05   6 5 4 3 2

Writing from the Heart is dedicated to the more than 60,000 young people around the world who have written a *laws of life* essay. May their words of wisdom reap a lifetime of blessings.

And to Becky Templeton, the very first "Contest Champion," whose 15-year commitment to the Franklin County Essay Contest is an inspiration to us all.

Contents

The order of the essays in this volume chronicles the growth of the Laws of Life *Essay Contest from the first contest in Tennessee launched in 1987 to the most recent contest in Nebraska that began in 2000.*

Foreword

Sir John Templeton congratulates high school senior Damion Forbes, who won Grand Prize in a Laws of Life *Essay Contest held in Nassau, Bahamas.*

Love. Forgiveness. Compassion. Honesty. Perseverance. These are universal values, timeless *laws of life* that transcend all cultures and religions. There are literally hundreds of these spiritual principles that guide us, whatever we do or wherever we go on our life's journey. But these "laws" can only guide us if we are aware of them, if we personalize and apply them to our own experience. In short, before we can live by the *laws of life,* we must discover them for ourselves.

How do we discover our own values, our own *laws of life?* I believe that each and every one of us can identify the set of principles we want to live by, if we reflect on the events we have passed through, the people we have known, and the lessons we have learned. By discovering and practicing these values, we have the power to transform our lives into more deeply useful and joyful experiences.

As a young boy growing up in Franklin County, Tennessee, I was privileged to receive abundant lessons on good character that were taught to me at home and school and were reinforced by example, through the behavior of my parents, my spiritual elders, and the members of my community. Very few doors were locked in my hometown. A person's word and handshake were sacred; and honesty was always the best policy. With so many models and examples of positive character, I was able to identify and practice the values by which I wanted to lead my life. I was given the freedom and the opportunity to discover my own *laws of life.*

The *Laws of Life* Essay Contest offers young people the same opportunity. In 1987, when we started the essay contest in Franklin County, it had an amazing effect on the county. Two things made it work. The first was the prizes. They ranged from $100 for honorable mention to $2,000 for the grand prize. The Franklin County students got terribly excited about winning cash prizes, and the idea swept the county. After a couple of years, three-quarters of the students were writing essays on their own values. The other principle of success was this: we did not tell the young people what to write about. We simply asked them to tell us in their own words! We all know that young people love to share their stories and reach their own conclusions. This is what the *Laws of Life* Essay Contest is all about: offering young people an opportunity to reflect and write about their beliefs and principles, and then publicly recognizing them for affirming the values by which they want to live.

Writing from the Heart celebrates these timeless principles and the children who have written about them. And it chronicles the astonishing growth of the essay contest from my hometown in Franklin County, Tennessee to communities around the world.

CELEBRATING OUR YOUNG PEOPLE

First and foremost, *Writing from the Heart* is a tribute to our young people. The 62 essays featured in the pages of this book illustrate the innate capacity for goodness within all young people, especially when they are encouraged to reflect upon the treasures they hold inside. From Chattanooga to China, the essays you will find in this book are all extraordinary. Moreover, they have been honored by their individual communities for the breadth of their ideas and the life lessons they contain.

The 62 essays printed in this book not only celebrate the accomplishments of their writers. They also exemplify the more than 60,000 young people around the world who have participated in a *Laws of Life* Essay Contest. Every one of the 60,000 essays is remarkable, and the writers are all winners—each of them authors of their own destiny.

Take your time as you read the essays in this book. You are being offered a rare opportunity to peer into the hearts of young people around the world. What you will learn about them will astound you. Each of the essays illustrates the personal journey taken by the writers as they reflect upon the experiences they have had and the people who have been most significant to them in their young lives. Many of the stories the writers share are uplifting. Some are very tragic. With openness and candor, the writers share their trials and triumphs, their everyday moments, their mistakes, and the lessons they have learned. Each of the essays bears witness to a transformation as the writers make sense of their values and beliefs, distilling them from the crucible of personal experience. As I read the essays I was greatly moved by some of the hardships that today's young people have had to face. Despite those challenges, the essays brim with optimism, faith in the future, and belief in oneself. The essays offer us not only a window into our young people's thoughts and beliefs. They inspire us to make the most of our own lives as well.

Although the writers discuss a variety of "laws," the wisdom they impart most often follows one of three types: 1) positive character traits that we should all strive to live by; 2) advice for how to make the most out of life; and 3) how we should behave toward others. The table below highlights the many different themes that the 62 young people chose to write about. (Each of the essays is listed by themes on page 185.)

FREQUENCY OF THEMES IN STUDENT ESSAYS

Positive Character Traits	Frequency	Principles for Successful Living	Frequency	Conduct Toward Others	Frequency
Love	6	Living Life to the Fullest	7	Helping Others	6
Optimism	5	Having Faith	4	Compassion	4
Honesty	4	Importance of Family	4	Kindness	4
Courage	3	Believing in Yourself	4	Respect	3
Perseverance	3	Living by Your Values	4	Forgiving Others	1
Patience	1	Having Integrity	3	Not Judging Others	1
Happiness	1	Importance of Learning	2	Being Fair	1
Redemption	1	Living Life Simply	2		
		Trying Your Hardest	1		

Note: *The number of themes exceeds the number of essays, because in a few essays students wrote about more than one* law of life.

Not surprisingly, the essays in this book illustrate that young people all over the world hold similar values and beliefs. As I read these essays, I was amazed at how universal these lessons are and how much we can learn from our young people.

THE ESSAY SELECTION PROCESS

The 62 essays that appear in this book were first written for one of the 54 *Laws of Life* Essay Contests launched in communities, schools, and programs all over the world. The John Templeton Foundation asked the sponsors of each contest to submit their first-place essay as well as two other top finalists from their most recent contest. From those three essays, the Foundation selected one essay to be featured in this book. With few exceptions, each of the essay contests is represented by its grand prizewinner.

Two programs deviated from the selection process. First, the Joseph Family Foundation sponsors individual contests in a number of southern California high schools. We chose to represent the scope of the Joseph Family Foundation contests by featuring five of their essays. Second, the I*EARN Essay Project involves 26 countries. In this program, students from all over the world participate in a cross-cultural dialogue as they share their essays on the Internet for everyone to enjoy. Prizes are not awarded to the writers, but in every other sense the five essays we featured from the I*EARN Essay Project are award-winning.

A CELEBRATION OF COMMUNITY SPIRIT

This book is a tribute to the business leaders, educators, community foundations, school districts, neighbors, parents, churches—all of the individuals and groups that have sponsored and organized essay contests in their communities and schools. The Listing of Contest Sponsors on page 180 illustrates the wide range of individuals and organizations that have launched essay contests around the world. To this day, as it was in my hometown, the contest remains a *local program*, financially sponsored and organized in the community in which it is held.

The order of the essays in this book chronicles the growth of the contest, beginning with the first contest in Franklin County, Tennessee on page 3 and pausing for now on page 174 with the newest contest launched in Omaha, Nebraska this past spring. The contest has spread mostly by word of mouth. Each one has been started by individuals who believe in the ideals and benefits of the program and that it will make a difference in the lives of children. To this date, 54 contests have been launched, in 23 states throughout the United States and in 30 countries around the world, including Russia, China, India, South Africa, Canada, and the United Kingdom. You can find out if there is an essay contest in your area by referring to the Listing of Contest Locations on page 179, which catalogues the contests by community, state, and country. (And if there isn't currently a contest where you live, I invite you to start one!)

Because the essay contest is locally sponsored and organized, each contest is unique, designed to fit the needs and spirit of its community and schools. In some cases, as for the West Philadelphia Catholic Contest on page 80, the program is adopted by one school. In others (e.g., the Mississippi Contest on page 21) the program is held statewide, with all schools invited to participate. Here are some other ways in which contests vary:

AGE – Many contests involve the participation of high school-aged students, but a large number of contests have also been started at the middle school level and in elementary schools. Indeed, the contest is intended for everyone: the young who each day are introduced to the values that will guide their lives, as well as the older and more experienced who seek confirmation and affirmation of their *laws of life*.

PRIZES – Most contests give cash prizes and certificates to their winners, from grand prize to honorable mention, and prize amounts vary greatly. In several contests, the winners receive a cash prize and a second cash award that they donate to the charity of their choice (see the Montgomery County Contest on page 18). Some contests award their winners cash prizes as well as partial college scholarships (see the Palm Beach County Contest on page 32).

FORM OF EXPRESSION – For most contests, participants are asked to express their *laws of life* in writing. However, in some communities, organizers have designed the contest so that students can illustrate their *laws of life* in other ways. For example, in the Guilford County Contest (see page 168), students are invited to express their *laws of life* using art, music, film, and photography, as well as writing.

Even the name of the contest can vary! "Write for Life," "Turning Points," "Values for Life"— these are all contests whose names have been chosen by their organizers to reflect the ideals and goals of the contest for their community.

As you read the essays in this book, imagine for a moment that the student writers live in your town or city, and that you are listening to them as they read their essays to an audience of parents, neighbors, teachers, and community leaders who have come together to honor them at the awards ceremony—and that *your* support helped make the contest possible.

Perhaps this book will inspire you to launch a *Laws of Life* Essay Contest in your community. Wouldn't it be a joy to provide your young people with an opportunity to think about love, kindness, friendship, forgiveness, and gratitude? The John Templeton Foundation offers a wide variety of contest materials and technical assistance to individuals and organizations interested in launching an essay contest. I encourage you to contact the Foundation so that you can learn more about the contest and how you can give the gift of character education to your community.

ACKNOWLEDGMENTS

Without the commitment and hard work of the hundreds of contest sponsors, organizers, volunteers, and parents, and all of the principals and teachers who support and administer the contest, this book would not have been possible. The *Laws of Life* Essay Contest has spread from town to town, thanks to the unflagging enthusiasm of individuals who hear about the essay contest and know right away that the program will benefit young people. Each year these "Contest Champions" bring their community and schools together to celebrate the young people who have thought carefully about the values that will guide their life.

The following Contest Champions helped in assembling the 62 essays, student photos and biographies, and contest profiles contained in *Writing from the Heart: Young People Share Their Wisdom:* Charlie Abourjilie, Dick Allen, Elizabeth Peale Allen, Nancy Andrew, Cathy Barrett, Janis Bean, John Beard, Aggie Becker, Berkley Bedell, Sheldon Benardo, Jack Bovee, Alicia Brennan, Sr. Mary Bur, Barry Burleson, Amy Butler, Bruce Cambigue, Vince Cancro, Lorraine Chambers, Rick Chambers, Larry Cockrum, Brenda Collins, Leo Collins, Sr. Ellen Convey, Dana Cooper, Lori Cranson, Jack Currier, Jon Dalton, John Davies, Anita Davis, Bonnie Davis, John Dodd, John Donaldson, Oscar Donkor, Corky Dow, Diane Drennan, Kathy Fell, Fred Foss, Leslie Frazee, Harvey Friedman, Paula Gavin, Kenneth Giniger, Ed Gragert, Mena Griffiths, Leo Hawk, Thomas Hill, Kathy Holman,

Thom Houghton, Deborah & Stuart Irby, Joe Irby, Jeff Jaffe, Janis Jarvis, Mrs. Worthington Johnson, Lynn Joseph, William King, Bela Kletnick, Nina Kuznetsova, Chris Larsen, Margie Legg, Jack Letvinchuk, Sarah Lucas, Angela Macias, Terri May, Suzi McCreery, Linda McKay, Rev. Hal Milton, Pat Nugent, Rev. Stephen Orchard, Pat Panzeca, Eileen Perra, Robert Rabon, Warren Romaine, Rev. Don Rose, Cynthia Rowan, Eileen Rueth, S.B. "Skeet" Rymer, Kent Sampson, Virginia Sampson, Neil Sawyer, Carl Schoenstedt, Jane Schuck, Bill Schuler, Bren Simon, Regina Smith, Kevin Smith-Fagan, Stelle Snyder, Marie Souder, Nan Starling, Jackie Strick, Becky and Handly Templeton, Pina Templeton, Robert Vitalo, Ashley Ward, Carolin Whitaker, Frederic Wolfe, Mary Wynn, and Rhonda Zimmerman.

I would like to express my deepest gratitude to each and every individual who has made this publication possible, so that others can read, enjoy, and learn from the wisdom found in its pages.

John Marks Templeton

WRITING FROM THE HEART

Kacey Mason
age 16

John Templeton *Laws of Life* Essay Contest
FRANKLIN COUNTY, TENNESSEE

on HELPING OTHERS
"In truth, giving is receiving"

As I RECALL MY CHILDHOOD, I vividly remember my mother constantly trying to help others. She gave food and clothes and also collected furniture for several different families who were relocating and starting over in an effort to leave the devastation of an abusive life behind. She gave countless hours of her time lending an ear, as well as an open heart, when there seemed to be no one else who could or would help. Often Mom would come home and help us go through our toys, especially those we seemed to have outgrown, for her many "other" children she was working with who had so little. Sometimes, she would take my older sister and me with her to the shelter where she gave so much of herself. There were always displaced little kids running around, looking for some attention. My sister and I took care of some of the kids while my mother talked to their mothers. Mom tried to ensure that the children in our community had a good Christmas, just like us. Her positive example helped me to realize the importance of helping others, keeping a good reputation, and maintaining a strong relationship with God.

I feel that we should all share with each other, whether it be material possessions or time. Wouldn't it be wonderful if we could all have the heart of Mother Teresa: Her whole life was dedicated to helping others less fortunate; she spent all of her time in selfless sacrifice. A simple gift of time brings such joy to others. Just spending an hour of time with a lonely person will give him tremendous joy. Also, the sharing of money, even though this is not the most important kind of sharing, can help somebody who needs clothes, food, or maybe even shelter. Calvin

Coolidge aptly remarked; "No person was ever honored for what he received. Honor has been the reward for what he gave."

There is only one thing you come into this world with that you also leave with —your name. I know that everything I do is a reflection of who I am. It is typical for others to remember the bad that we do more than they do the good. The positive contributions and helpful advice donated by my mother that I have not only seen for myself, but also heard about from others, have been a helpful influence in all I do. Seeing the faces of the many people she's helped and the positive outcome of what first seemed impossible makes me strive to help others in any way possible. I always want my name to reflect my positive influence. Shakespeare also recognized the importance of a good reputation:

> Good name in man and woman, dear my Lord,
> Is the immediate jewel of their souls…
> But he that filches from me my good name
> Robs me of that which not enriches him and makes me poor indeed.

My decision to do right is also guided by my relationship with God through prayer and reading my Bible. By doing so, I have learned many valuable lessons. Luke 6:31 says, "Do unto others as you would have them do unto you." Through my reading I have learned the importance of kindness toward everyone. When I apply this to the way I live my life, I can see that people do profit from someone else's kindness. When I am generous and go out of my way for other people, my day seems more pleasant. I believe that kindness has a very positive effect on both me and my peers. I think it is very important to read God's word and keep a relationship with Him. I wake up every morning, knowing that whatever the day ahead of me holds, He will be with me. I will always have His unconditional love to guide me.

I have realized that it is not important what I do for myself, but instead what I do for others. I have achieved much through my Christian morals of giving, keeping a good reputation, and being kind to others. In truth, giving is receiving. However, if one is thinking of receiving while giving, the blessing is lost. In 1962, Martin Luther King stated, "The universe is so structured that things do not quite work out rightly if men are not diligent in their concern for others…. All life is interrelated." I know that if I continue to live my life this way, I will be happy and accomplish my goals.

Kacey plans to graduate from college with a degree in physical therapy or athletic train-ing. "Before the contest I never really thought about my morals and goals," she explains. "This opportunity has helped me understand and relay to others how important it is to think about our values."

⌒

JOHN TEMPLETON *LAWS OF LIFE* ESSAY CONTEST

In 1986, Sir John Templeton received the key to Franklin County, Tennessee in a cere-mony attended by the Governor and other distinguished officials. To thank the county for bestowing him with such an honor, he gave to the citizens of Franklin County a promise: he would sponsor a bi-annual essay contest to encourage young people to write about their own *laws of life*. The essay contest has been a major highlight of the county's school year ever since. Since its inception in 1987, the contest has been administered by Becky and Handly Templeton, Sir John's niece and nephew. Combining the fall and spring contests, over 1,500 young people in Franklin County write a *laws of life* essay each year. Franklin County is proud that over the years winners have emerged from all levels of academic abil-ities. This encourages all students to participate and to have confidence that they may win a major prize.

Over 20 cash prizes are given out annually. The grand prizewinners in both the fall and spring contests receive $2,000. In addition, the teacher of the grand prizewinner receives $300. Five county schools participate in the contest: Franklin County High School, Hunt-land High School, H. Louis Scott Junior High School, J.D. Jackson Junior High School, and St. Andrews-Sewanne School.

In 1997, the essay contest expanded to eight elementary schools in Franklin County. Teachers at the schools select character traits that are important to both students and the community as a whole. Every six weeks, students discuss one of these qualities in their individual classrooms. At the end of each six-week period, a student is selected who best exemplifies the character trait. The student receives a certificate, a *laws of life* pencil, and a free pizza and coke from the local Domino's Pizza.

"Those of us in Franklin County," says Becky Templeton, "know that one of Sir John's greatest legacies will be his concern for character education in our county, his hometown of Winchester, Tennessee." ✷

Arjay Velasco
age 13

The Giniger Award
for Excellence in Writing

BRONX, NEW YORK

on OPTIMISM
"Standing high on the peaks of life"

NUMEROUS PEOPLE have positive attitudes that help them in many ways. They can help them get through life's many difficulties or life's many decisions. In this essay, I will share the positive attitudes I take with me everywhere I go.

A positive attitude I always take with me is the attitude of knowing I can succeed in anything. This gives me the strength and power I need. It helps me to overcome the days when I feel so stressed out about school. It helps me to go on to do my work and is the main key to my motivation. It is very important that we show an attitude that is both positive and appropriate—an attitude that speaks for who we are and something that gives us character and personality.

The attitude that I can succeed in anything has helped me in life too. It gives me the courage that any decisions I make will take me through life. It has also given to me the most uplifting respect for myself. I have learned that failure is not a defeat but an inspiration to do better.

Another positive attitude I take with me is the attitude of knowing that tomorrow is another day—a whole new day of adventure and surprises. This attitude helps me in times of difficulties and the times when everything in my world goes wrong. This attitude helps me overcome those obstacles. It has given me all the confidence in the world. It has given me the opportunity to never look back at yesterday. I now view yesterday as the past, and know that a brighter tomorrow and future will come my way.

Before we can stand up high on the peaks of life, we should have the attitude of loving ourselves for who we are. Having this positive attitude indicates the starting line of our future, a future that will reveal itself. One must remember never to give up on life since it has so much to offer.

In having this positive attitude you will be successful in life and in all the decisions you make in life.

Arjay is a Summerbridge Scholar and will attend the Summerbridge Program for the next two years. His goal is to study at an Ivy League university and become a doctor. Arjay shares that "Writing an essay based on a law of life *is something everyone should do. I truly believe in what I wrote."*

∽

THE GINIGER AWARD FOR EXCELLENCE IN WRITING
Renee Giniger Feingold, Evelyn Giniger Hoffman and Kenneth Giniger, former graduates of P.S.86 in the Bronx, NY, decided that they would make a lasting contribution to the elementary school that had provided them with so many happy memories. In the spring of 1995, they began sponsoring the first Grade 6 Giniger Award for Excellence in Writing, which has since become an annual event.

Bela Kletnick, Writing Staff Developer, coordinates the yearlong writing program with the enthusiastic support of Principal Sheldon Benardo. Assigned topics focus on personal values and goal setting, and the essays are written using the writing process strategies of prewriting, drafting, revising, editing, and publication. Approximately 300 students participate in the program. A spring awards ceremony honors the nine finalists, and the three top winners receive a $50 savings bond. The Giniger family presents every finalist with a book, and teachers are also acknowledged with a gift of appreciation. This annual writing assembly has become a memorable event significant to the entire school community.

"My sisters and I sponsor the writing awards program," shares Kenneth Giniger, "in thanks for the education we received at P.S. 86, and to encourage today's students to become interested in writing." ✴

Leah Webber
age 9

Guideposts for Kids Magazine
Laws of Life Essay Contest
CARMEL, NEW YORK

on LOVE
"Sometimes to love means to sacrifice"

THAT IS SOMETHING I have heard my mom say from time to time, but I never really understood what it meant until a couple of years ago. It all began one cold January night...

I woke up to crying! I ran into my sister Caley's room... she said her head hurt really badly. I ran downstairs to get my parents. Caley was taken to a nearby hospital. She was delirious! The doctor sent her in a helicopter quick! To a hospital two hours away! There my parents learned Caley had a brain aneurysm—kind of like bleeding inside the brain. That was very serious! For three weeks Mom stayed at the hospital with Caley. I had to sacrifice my time with Mom.... I had to sacrifice a lot! I love my sister; and I kept reminding myself that Caley needed Mom more than I did. Sometimes to love means to sacrifice.

When Caley and Mom came home from the hospital, I was so glad to see them. Then, my parents asked me if I would share my bedroom with Caley (my room is closest to my parents' room) so they could hear her at night. Truthfully, I really wanted a room of my own, but I love my sister, so I said, "Sure." Sometimes to love means to sacrifice.

During the past two and a half years, since Caley's brain aneurysm, she has had a lot of physical restrictions... she can't do anything that might increase her blood pressure or jolt her, causing her another brain bleed. (Things such as running, jumping, going upside down, and holding her breath, Caley cannot do.) Many times when I was playing with Caley, I chose not to do those things so Caley

wouldn't feel bad. I wanted to play like an ordinary kid, but I love my sister and...
sometimes to love means to sacrifice.

Our family hasn't even gone to any amusement parks during these past two and
a half years because Caley isn't allowed to ride any rides. Sure, I'd like to go, but I
love my sister. Sometimes to love means to sacrifice.

But guess what? My sister is getting better! Soon we will be able to do lots of fun
activities again. Through the past two and a half years, my sister Caley (who is two
years older than me) and I have grown closer and closer. I love my sister. Sometimes
to love means to sacrifice. And she is worth it. Now it actually feels like it was no
sacrifice at all.

*Leah likes being home-schooled because her mom makes learning fun. She shares that
"Writing a* laws of life *essay has been a life changing experience for me. More than anything, I am thankful to share with the readers of my essay the wonderful miracle God
performed in my sister's life. Hopefully readers will see how important it is for families
to stick together through hard times."*

<hr>

GUIDEPOSTS FOR KIDS MAGAZINE *LAWS OF LIFE* ESSAY CONTEST

The idea to feature the essay contest in the *Guideposts for Kids* magazine grew out of an old
friendship between Sir John Templeton and Norman and Ruth Peale.

Since 1995, the contest has been held once a year for the magazine's readers and is open
to all children between the ages of seven and twelve. Thousands of kids have written a
laws of life essay and submitted it to the *Guideposts for Kids* Essay Contest, and close to one
thousand children participated in the contest this past year. Each year, the grand prizewinner receives $5,000.

"Sir John and my parents shared the same goal, of bringing a better and fuller life to as
many people as possible," says Elizabeth Peale Allen. "I hope that everyone who enters the
contest or reads the winning essays in *Guideposts* is moving toward a more rewarding
life." ✸

Ashlee Cook
age 18

Bradley County *Laws of Life* Essay Contest
BRADLEY COUNTY, TENNESSEE

on FORGIVING OTHERS
"Nothing should keep us from forgiving each other"

"LIFE IS NOT FAIR" is a quotation that was often relayed to me as a growing adolescent. My parents always used this statement to quiet me after I had unsuccessfully tried to argue my way into getting something that I felt I needed. As I matured, I came to the conclusion that life was more unfair than I could ever imagine. This helped me to discover an important *law of life*: forgiveness.

The phone ringing after ten o'clock was not common at my house. So, naturally I was shocked when a startling ring occurred at 12:15 a.m. on August 7, 1999. As I answered the call hurriedly, I heard a voice from a staff member of the Erlanger Hospital. The nurse asked if this was the residence that she had assumed it was. I confirmed her assumption as my entire body became paralyzed from fright. She kept our conversation brief as she just said that my father had been in an accident and she would give me further details when I came to the hospital. Every possibility of what could have happened that night came involuntarily into my mind. Agreeing with my mother that it would be best if I looked after my siblings, she would begin the most difficult journey of her life. Hours after her departure, my mother returned home with a few close family members. She gathered my brother, sister, and me together to give us what we felt to be the most unrealistic news. My stepfather had been pronounced dead at 10:07 p.m. the previous evening.

Searching inside myself, looking for answers, became the only action I could perform. Taking into consideration that something happened that I could not change, that I could not control just absolutely, pierced my heart to the point of no healing. While trying to cope with the newborn loss of part of my humanity, I observed the reactions of everyone around me. All of my family, while saddened seemed to share one common emotion otherwise—anger. They were all so enraged that the carelessness of a 26-year-old college student had taken away someone they loved wholeheartedly. It seemed that I almost did not fit in. As I kept seeing the emotions of a bitter and vengeful family, their reactions brought me even lower. I thought about how a young lady did take away something from three people on the night of August 6, 1999 that she could never give back—life. At this point a new clarity took over me. How could my family and I forget the one person who would also have to live with this the rest of her life? Of course, I am implying that this person is the driver of the vehicle that killed my father. As my mind became clouded with contradicting oppositions, I brought myself to write the following:

Ever since I had been born I knew we'd pass away
But I can't grasp the reality of why he went that day
Perspective has been set to my otherwise petty views
Sometimes you take for granted just how much you have to lose
The motto of "living for the day" passes with the sunrise of the next
So every day at dawn you begin a brand new text
Every single day is a chapter of your life
Whether it be exciting, sad, or filled with strife
Daddy didn't decide that he wanted to go that day
But even as strong as he was he just couldn't get his way
There's no doubt he loved me even though we fought quite a few times
Daddy had his faults just like I have all of mine
I know he hung on to tell us just once more
How much that he loved us in the life he lived before
Daddy was a strong one; he taught me to be the same
He never loved me any less even though we had different names
I guess if I was asked I would do things differently
But I wouldn't change the relationship that Daddy had with me
Because we were so much alike, sometimes it was hard to get along
Decisions took a while with us because both of us were "never" wrong
Values have been instilled in me that I will never forget
I'll use them everyday until my creator and I have met
So many people ask me "why aren't you mad?"
I answer them, "I don't have time when I am so sad."
I have forgiven the one who is responsible by the world

How could I do anything else but feel sorry for that girl
She has made a mistake that will haunt her for all her life
Maybe it wouldn't be that way if she were more careful that night
So please forgive that girl who all this happened to
After all wouldn't you want to be forgiven if that girl was you?

Forgiveness is too easily spoken of, but not so easily carried out. Experiencing such tragedy has strengthened my execution of forgiveness toward others and myself. As a college bound senior, I have been faced with the most difficult trials of my life in the past seven months. But I have been grateful for all of them. How could this be? God has explained that testing of faith makes us stronger and more devout Christians. He never leads us into situations that we cannot overcome with His help. He *NEVER* gives us more than we can handle! Two days after the loss of my father, my aunt spoke of me in front of friends of the family and said, "this is the girl who will hold our family together." I constantly hear the echoes of my aunt's quotation in my head, reminding me that I am thought of as my family's strength. I have been strengthened by God and it evidently has shone through me to others. If I maintain God's will, then soon my family will see forgiveness in me too. Hopefully, God will let them see that everyone makes mistakes, and we all need forgiveness to move ahead in life.

There is no excuse in the world that should hinder us from forgiving others. It is not always easy. But the times when it is most difficult for us to follow through are usually when your forgiveness is treasured most. Do not let the small things (or large things) keep you angry—it is not worth it. Nothing should keep us from forgiving each other.

Ashlee plans to attend Lipscomb University in Nashville, Tennessee, where she will double major in vocal music and psychology. She would like to thank her teacher, Ms. Amanda Jackson, for encouraging her and her classmates to be their best every day.

BRADLEY COUNTY *LAWS OF LIFE* ESSAY CONTEST

For a great idea to take off, sometimes all you need is a few good friends. That's exactly what happened when S.B. "Skeet" Rymer, an old friend of Sir John Templeton and former CEO of the Magic Chef Corporation, brought the essay contest to Bradley County, Tennessee. The contest was first launched in the spring of 1995. To this day, Mr. and Mrs. Rymer financially sponsor the contest. Since its inception, the contest has been effectively administered in the local schools by Cleveland Associated Industries (C.A.I.), an organization that supports business growth and educational programs in Bradley County.

This past year, 1,100 essays were received from seven area schools: Bradley Central High, Bradley Junior High, Charleston, Cleveland High, Cleveland Middle, Horizon, and Trewhitt Junior High. Twenty junior and senior high students were honored at a reception held at the Cleveland Country Club, where 100 guests, including the mayor and the police chief, were in attendance. The students won cash prizes totaling over $8,900.

When asked why they continue to sponsor the contest, Mr. and Mrs. Rymer replied, "We think every person has a responsibility to the community in which he lives to make it better. We really believe that the *Laws of Life* Essay Contest is a genuine educational help in Bradley County." ✳

Peter Blair
age 15

Bahamas *Laws of Life* Essay Contest
BAHAMAS

on HONESTY
"Is honesty still the best policy?"

A "LAW OF LIFE" is a moral value or principle by which one may choose to govern his or her behavior, attitude and life in general. Moreover, it may be a belief that is religious in nature, to which one adheres and utterly respects. Also, it is quite similar to a law of the land, in that it is to be followed at all cost. Hence, without such constraints, the quality of our lives would immensely diminish.

It so happened that I was in a food store with my mother, when a little boy had been caught trying to steal a chocolate bar. Eventually, the news spread throughout the entire shop, and a crowd of people began congregating around the boy. His abashed mother could no longer hide behind her rough exterior, and very soon, she experienced an emotional outburst, which included tears of sorrow, disappointment and shame. All of the bystanders sympathized with the child, who seemed to be upset because he knew that he had caused his single parent mother her public disgrace. The remorseful boy made a sincere apology to both the general manager of the store and his mother for the bad deed that he had perpetrated. Aware of the current circumstances, the general manager smiled and then handed the boy the chocolate bar. He then said, "I'll let you off free this time, only because you did the right thing and told the truth." The store rocked with excitement as the people cheered wildly in support of the decision to grant mercy to the young child. At that instant, it hit me I should write about honesty as a *law of life*.

"Honesty" is synonymous with the old saying: "Honesty is the best policy." This was true in the case of the boy in the story, as his honesty granted him forgiveness from the general manager and the acceptance of the people. Furthermore, this event, which showed him the importance of honesty, may also help to steer his life in the right direction, while helping him to develop character.

The Bible also emphasizes the significance of integrity to God in the following passage of scripture.

> Finally, brethren, whatsoever things are true, whatsoever things are honest, whatsoever things are just, whatsoever things are pure, whatsoever things are lovely, whatsoever things are of good report; if there be any virtue, and if there be any praise, think on these things. (Philippians 4:8 KJV)

This very vivid and accurate scripture clearly outlines what God expects from his people. Furthermore, honesty is mentioned second as one of the necessary criteria for the things upon which God wants us to meditate. Therefore, we can safely say that honesty is of paramount importance to God.

In today's modern society, unscrupulous businessmen, drug dealers, conniving politicians and white-collared thieves are thriving financially. They also are in constant fear for they know not when their sins will find them out, as they are often running from the law, which they are continuously breaking. Meanwhile, the vast majority of the morally upright citizens live in dire poverty and are barely making ends meet. To me, this is one of the greatest parodies that exists in normal everyday life. Also, it is the epitome of irony. If honesty is indeed the best policy then why are corrupt people prospering whereas the honest people are often struggling? This is a frequently asked question by those persons who want to be good citizens. The Bible clearly underscores the short-term success of dishonest people on numerous occasions. In addition, the Bible urges us not to get preoccupied with earthly gain, but rather those things that pertain to the spiritual.

> Lay not up for yourselves treasures upon earth, where moth and rust doth corrupt, and where thieves break through and steal: But lay up for yourselves treasures in heaven, where neither moth nor rust doth corrupt, and where thieves do not break through nor steal: For where your treasure is, there will your heart be also. (Matt. 6:19-21 KJV)

These scriptures show us the fragility of materialistic things, as they will all eventually deteriorate or become useless and redundant. Finally, all of the headaches and pain that accompany dishonest gain are not worth one's sanity and peace of mind.

Furthermore, if we were all honest in every aspect of our lives, the world would be a much better place. Firstly, there would be no crime or wars. Secondly, racism would be a thing of the past as well as gender inequality. Thirdly, our honesty toward each other would eradicate all jealousy, envy or covetousness, as we would want what is ours and only ours. Finally, family ties would be strengthened, as there would be no more secrets between parents and their children. For these reasons, it is quite obvious that living an honest and morally acceptable life is one of the most fulfilling and satisfying feelings that anyone can ever experience.

It should now be crystal clear to you that honesty is still the best policy, as dishonesty only brings about unnecessary burdens in these already stressful and perilous times. In conclusion the challenge awaits us all; live honestly and avoid having a lifetime of regrets.

After graduating from high school, Peter plans to study business at a university in the United States. "Participating in such a positive event in our nation has really enriched me as an individual," he shares. "It has given me more confidence as a writer, which has resulted in a vast improvement in my writing and reading comprehension skills."

❧

BAHAMAS *LAWS OF LIFE* ESSAY CONTEST

The Bahamas Contest began in the spring of 1995 and is open to all Bahamas schools, public and private. The contest is sponsored by investment counselor John Donaldson, a longtime friend of Sir John Templeton.

One significant component of the contest is a Kick-Off Event for English teachers. Working with the Ministry of Education, the event is a wonderful way for teachers to learn more about the contest. "This event has really had an impact on the success of the contest," says Mena Griffiths, who coordinates the Bahamas Essay Contest.

This past year, students from 45 different Bahamas schools wrote a *laws of life* essay. The awards ceremony was held at the Buena Vista Hotel and was attended by over 100 people, including John Donaldson, Sir John Templeton, and a distinguished official from the Ministry of Education. More than $5,500 in prizes was awarded to 14 students, and the two grand prizewinners each won $1,500.

At the awards ceremony, teachers whose students participate in the contest are also recognized with a special raffle. Each year, one lucky teacher is awarded two free airline tickets to anywhere in the United States.

"One of the most important principles to learn in life is that hard work is the first step to achieving personal success," shares John Donaldson. "The earlier in life that one learns this principle, the greater chance one has of realizing personal success. I got involved with the *Laws of Life* Essay Contest because it does such a wonderful job of instilling this principle in young people." ✳

Andrew Gilman
age 12

Montgomery County
Laws of Life Essay Contest

MONTGOMERY COUNTY, NORTH CAROLINA

on COURAGE
"Let me show courage in everything I do"

WEBSTER'S COLLEGIATE DICTIONARY defines courage as "mental or moral strength to venture, persevere, and withstand danger, fear, or difficulty." The history of our world is filled with people who have demonstrated tremendous courage.

What would our world be like today if Christopher Columbus had not had the courage to search for new worlds and dare to venture where others dared not to go? What if our ancestors had not found the courage to venture to a new land to find the freedom to worship and live as they desperately wanted? What if Neil Armstrong did not find the courage to explore space and walk on the moon? Men and women who dared to venture into uncharted territory displayed phenomenal courage to help our lives be better, and I am grateful.

What would our world be like today if Martin Luther King, Jr. had not found the courage to persevere in the non-violent struggle to secure equality for all races? What if the Jewish people did not find the courage to persevere through the horrible times during the Holocaust? What if Jackie Robinson failed to find the courage to remain with the Brooklyn Dodgers even as he was taunted and subjected to racial slurs? Again, our world is a better place today because we have had these people of courage to do what's right and in doing so become role models for us all.

However, there are millions of courageous people with whom we come in contact every day that can show us what true courage is. They may never be in our history books, we may never see them on the 7:00 news shows, or we may not read about them in the newspapers, but their acts of courage are just as inspiring. A little girl of three years of age who goes to my church was diagnosed with liver cancer. Throughout all her chemotherapy treatments which made her very sick and lose all of her hair, she still smiled and laughed and made the rest of us do the same. That took courage. I also know a boy who was born with arms shorter than normal but still excels in any kind of sport. That takes courage and determination, too.

In middle school everyone wants to belong and be part of the group. Sometimes it takes courage to go against the group if what they're doing is wrong. If my friends and I refuse to make fun of someone because they don't wear the high priced shoes or brand name clothes that the "in crowd" wears it takes courage, but I know it's right. If I refuse to "put down" someone because of the color of her skin, his height or weight, or the way she walks or talks, it takes courage, but again I know it is right. It takes courage for youth to say no to others who offer them drugs, alcohol or tobacco. Every day we encounter problems that take courage to solve in a way that will benefit ourselves and others.

The poet, Adam Lindsey Gordon (1833–1870) wrote,

> Life is mostly froth and bubble,
> Two things stand like stone
> Kindness in another's trouble
> Courage in our own.

I hope throughout my life I will find the courage as I face trouble and difficulties to do the right thing. I may or may not be as courageous as those I read about in my history books but I hope to show courage in doing what's right every day of my life. In the book of Joshua, Chapter 1, Verse 6 it says "Be strong and of a good courage." It's such a simple statement, but the responsibility is strong: Let me show courage in everything I do.

Andrew's favorite activities include baseball, football, swimming, and being with his friends. He believes his teacher, Mr. Arlester Simpson, is the kind of person who lives the laws of life every day.

MONTGOMERY COUNTY *LAWS OF LIFE* ESSAY CONTEST

Read any good books lately? In the summer of 1995, while reading Sir John Templeton's book *Discovering the Laws of Life,* Warren Romaine "discovered" the essay contest. He knew right away that this was a project worth undertaking. Mr. Romaine approached a friend at the local bank, First Bancorp, with the idea of co-sponsoring the contest in Montgomery County, North Carolina. And so the contest was off and running!

The first year of the contest drew over 1,000 entries. Each year, a grand prizewinner is chosen along with two winners from each school that participates. In addition to a cash prize, the top winners also receive $500 to donate to the charity of their choice—what a wonderful way to teach young people about the joy of giving.

The spring of 2000 marked the fifth year of the contest. Every year, the awards are presented at a banquet held at a clubhouse next to a beautiful lake. The press covers the event in both print and on local television. For Warren Romaine, the most special part of the contest is the culminating event. "At the awards ceremony each year," he explains, "the winners and their families, teachers, judges, and special guests become one happy family. By the end of the evening, we all go home enriched in spirit." ✳

claire Nettles
age 17

Mississippi Statewide
Laws of Life Essay Contest

STATE OF MISSISSIPPI

on HELPING OTHERS
"Learning to give"

IN THE UNITED STATES we have many material blessings available to us. However, oftentimes we do not share those blessings with others. While on a trip to Romania I learned a very important *law of life:* give of yourself and your possessions every chance you have.

During July of 1999, I, along with eight others, traveled to the country of Romania to build a chapel in a Romanian/Hungarian village called Chet (Ketz). The town in which we stayed, Satu Mare, was filled with gypsies begging on tile streets. The road we traveled on the two hour bus ride to the village was lined with small two-room houses which house entire families. The same housing situation existed in Chet.

When we arrived in Chet the people of the village greeted us with broad smiles, anticipating the coming week. In Romania if a church does not have a building in which to worship, it is considered a cult. By going to the village and building the chapel we were making their church "legal." The people of the village were very thankful, more thankful than we realized.

The team came prepared to make lunches of sandwiches and salads all week. However, the first day we were on the building site the ladies of the village brought a home-cooked meal at lunchtime. Then they informed us that they would prepare lunch for us every day, an extremely generous offer. They have no air conditioning and in the summer, cooking around a hot fire is not very comfortable. Also, they don't have much money to buy food for a large group. These lunches were truly gifts of love. We were giving them something they needed, and they gave us something back.

However, their giving did not end with food. On the last day of work, the leader of the church called all the workers together and began a ceremony. He expressed his gratitude and asked us to remember Chet in our prayers. Then he presented every worker with a handmade gift, a mat of woven material, white, blue, green, red, purple, black, and yellow. The women of the village had once again given of their time, energy, and resources to thank a group of people who had come to help them.

Although the people of Chet do not know this, they gave me much more than food and a rug. They taught me a *law of life*. I am a person who is blessed beyond my imagination. I have a wonderful family, full of love and care. I have everything I need: food, clothing, and shelter; even the extras I desire. However, even when given the opportunities I fail to share these blessings like I should. As a recipient of the giving spirit of the people of Chet I now realize the importance of giving of myself and my possessions, even when it requires a sacrifice.

Claire has received numerous academic awards and plans to attend a four-year college. She is very active in her church where she participates in volunteer work and the youth praise band.

ᴈ

MISSISSIPPI STATEWIDE *LAWS OF LIFE* ESSAY CONTEST

At the end of each piece of music that Johann Sebastian Bach composed, he would write "S.D.G." or Soli Deo Gloria, which in Latin means "for the glory of God alone." The Soli Deo Gloria Foundation, a private philanthropy founded in 1995 by Stuart C. Irby, Jr., a Jackson, Mississippi businessman, has three goals, one of which is to promote and implement the *Laws of Life* Essay Contest.

After the contest's pilot year, the Soli Deo Gloria Foundation teamed up with the Mississippi High School Activities Association (MHSAA), an organization of 280 public schools across the state. MHSAA contest coordinator Betty Whitlock explains that the organization was interested in the program because, "It is one of the few essay contests where students decide what topic they want to write about."

The philosophy at Soli Deo Gloria is that every young person who takes the time to think and write about his or her *laws of life* is a winner, and that is why every student who writes an essay receives a complementary hardback copy of Sir John Templeton's book *Worldwide Laws of Life*.

Why have Stuart and Deborah Irby championed the essay contest for the last six years? Deborah Irby explains, "We sponsor the contest because we believe that all of us need to give serious attention to the values that we deem to be important." ✳

Kwonneung (Stephen) Kim
age 19

YMCA *Values in Life* Essay Contest
NEW YORK, NEW YORK

on HONESTY AND RESPECT
"Teaching the values that matter most"

LIFE IS UNPREDICTABLE. Before the start of the summer, I had no idea that I would be a YMCA summer camp counselor. Now, here I am near the end of the summer, finishing up camp. I can't say it's been easy, but it was undoubtedly a beneficial, enjoyable experience for me.

The children I helped take care of were very energetic. They were so playful. I found out that kids never run out of energy. We could come back from a full day of swimming at Rockland Pool, and they'd still want to play dodge ball. It took a lot of strength and effort on my part to keep up with them.

Sure, camp was meant for the kids to have fun, but the YMCA camp went beyond that and instilled values in the kids. This was a process I enjoyed implementing. Children need values in life and the YMCA promoted four main values. They were respect, responsibility, honesty, and caring.

I remember a time I tested the honesty of the kids. At camp, we had gone over each of the four values. I knew the kids knew them, but would they practice them? Once a girl in my group found a quarter. She was honest and gave it to me, telling me that it wasn't hers. I went to ask the kids whose quarter it was. At once, all of the kids jumped up and down laughing, saying, "mine, mine." Then I asked them if they were being honest, reminding them that it was one of the four values. One by one, the kids admitted that the quarter was not theirs. Finally, one child said that it was his and two other kids agreed with his statement, saying that they had witnessed him dropping it. I thanked all of them for their honesty and reminded them how important it was to be honest.

Respect and responsibility are two values which are difficult to implement. My children were part of the Break Aways program, sponsored by the Board of Education. One of the main goals of this program was to improve students' literacy skills. I really enjoyed the experience of teaching the children in this program, and felt as though I gained something from it. The children in this group were a challenge to work with. They would be very hyper before beginning an activity. But, once I started reading them a story or got them started on an activity, I had their undivided attention. Many times the kids would be reluctant to be quiet when it was time. But, by teaching them the value of respect, they became silent for me and other children when it was needed. They also learned to respect their peers. Without the value of respect, children grow up lacking dignity. This can ultimately cause chaos within a society.

I recall an incident in which I read the children a story and they loved it. In fact, I didn't even have to ask them what the moral of the story was. The kids started telling me themselves. They told me, "The story is trying to say that it doesn't matter how you look on the outside, but it's your heart on the inside that counts." They continued to tell me that if you have a dream you should never give up on that dream, no matter what obstacles lie in front of you. I was moved. I was in awe of how the kids learned all about caring and responsibility through a story I had read them. I congratulated them on their insights. I felt as though I was becoming a teacher.

The kids are not the only ones who learned from summer camp. I think we, as counselors, have learned a lot from children. I've noticed that children overcome tempers and conflicts quickly. They often realize that the solution is as simple as talking things through, or considering how the other person feels. It would be great if the world were like that. But, for a short summer, these children were exposed to four values that, if practiced, could help them for the rest of their lives. I certainly hope I will be part of the reason that they remember and apply these values.

Stephen is a Presidential Scholar at Baruch College, and he is a member of Phi Eta Sigma, a national honor society. "Participating in the essay contest was truly a joyful experience," he shares. "It enabled me to express my thoughts and insights in a clear, lucid way."

YMCA *VALUES IN LIFE* ESSAY CONTEST

In 1995, the YMCA of Greater New York established four core values to guide the organization: respect, responsibility, honesty, and caring. Under the leadership of executive director Paula Gavin, the YMCA implemented the essay contest as a way to highlight the importance of these values for camp counselors, most of whom are college students.

At the end of each summer, counselors from all 55 day camp sites are invited to write an essay about how they incorporated the four core values into their daily camp activities. The top 19 essays are submitted to a panel of YMCA staff and volunteer judges, who select three top prizewinners. Participants are awarded cash prizes totaling $5,000. Now in its fifth year, the *Values in Life* Essay Contest continues to be a thriving success! ✳

Ashley Cowan
age 17

Lima *Laws of Life* Essay Contest
LIMA, OHIO

on LIVING BY YOUR VALUES
"The laws of life will guide you through the roughest times"

The *laws of life* that you should abide,
Will guide you through the roughest times.
Through all the hate and senseless crimes,
In a world where little is sanctified.
With love and peace
And God in mind,
The answers desired, you will find.

If a soul is empty and so hollow,
Happiness is buried in its shadow.
A life of prosperity you will not know,
If you choose not to live by the laws that follow.

Without prejudice
And hate in your heart,
A life of fulfillment is bound to start.

THE LAWS OF LIFE

1. Listen to those for whom you care.
2. Be thoughtful and giving, cooperate and share.
3. Hold your values true and high.
4. Strive for your goals, with the limit the sky.

5. Study hard and be your best.
6. Set your standards above the rest.
7. Remember there's no "I" in team.
8. Imagine, don't be afraid to dream.
9. Help someone that you don't know.
10. Remember the heritage from which you grow.
11. Stand up for what you think is right.
12. Be selective and passionate for what you fight.
13. Let your closest friends know that you care.
14. Stay strong when things get hard to bear.
15. Fill your life with light and love.
16. Surround yourself with God above!

The *laws of life* that you should abide,
Will guide you through the roughest times.
Through all the hate and senseless crimes,
In a world where little is sanctified.
With love and peace
And God in mind,
The answers desired, you will find.
When all a person knows is anger,
His life is filled with hate and disaster.
Let God's words be your master,
And your soul will not succumb to danger.
If you live with love
And love living,
The life you lead will be fulfilling.

Ashley plans to attend Ohio State University. She believes her teacher, Ms. Bush, is a true role model who has earned her greatest respect. "Writing the laws of life *essay has made me realize what is most important in my life," Ashley adds. "The contest is a great chance for America's youth to speak their minds and be heard."*

LIMA *LAWS OF LIFE* ESSAY CONTEST

Since the 1996–1997 school year, the H&H Foundation, a family philanthropy established by Leo Hawk and Henry Hawk, Jr., has sponsored the Lima Contest. Leo Hawk heard about the essay contest from his friend Fritz Wolfe (who sponsors a contest in Hickory, North Carolina) and contacted Sir John Templeton to learn more about the program.

The H&H Foundation soon decided that the contest was a natural fit for Lima, a close-knit and supportive community located in western Ohio. Since its inception, Dick Scherger, formerly with the Lima city school system, has coordinated the program in the following schools: Apollo Career Center, Bath, Delphos Jefferson, Delphos St. John High School, Lima Central Catholic, Elida, Lima Senior, Perry, Shawnee, and Temple Christian.

Now in its fourth year, the Lima Contest has become a much anticipated community event, and this past year, 2,240 students submitted a *laws of life* essay. The awards banquet was held at Lima's Civic Center, and more than 400 guests attended the banquet, including the mayor, a state representative, and a local news crew. At this year's banquet, 91 students were awarded cash prizes totaling over $12,000!

Why have Leo Hawk and his family remained so committed to the essay contest? Explains Mr. Hawk, "We are all beacons of light for each other, and by encouraging young students to look at their *laws of life*, their beacons can shine on for generations." ✳

william Barrie
age 12

Fairfield Country Day School
Laws of Life Essay Contest
FAIRFIELD, CONNECTICUT

on KINDNESS AND BELIEVING IN YOURSELF
"To thine own self be true"

ALMOST EVERY DAY I have to make choices and decisions that reflect on my character—sometimes only to myself and sometimes to others, including my family, teachers, and friends. I want to be satisfied with myself and my decisions and to feel that I have made good choices. Whether my decisions or actions are impulsive or well thought out, I think they are based on what my conscience tells me is right. I believe my conscience has been influenced and formed mainly by my family. Fortunately, I have two good parents and an adult brother and sister who all share their good values with me by their example and by giving advice. There are two major *laws of life* that influence my decisions to do the right thing.

First of all, my mother has told me that her dad defined the word "gentleman" as someone who never intentionally hurts someone else's feelings. I have tried to use this as one of my ethics or rules of life. I really try hard not to laugh when someone else does or says something I think is dumb. Also, I try to make a point of not putting people down or gossiping about them. Sometimes this is really tough, especially when I want to retaliate against someone who has made fun of me or made me angry. When I am especially tempted to be mean to someone, I remind myself that I share my late grandfather's name and then try to be a "gentleman." I'm certainly not perfect at following this ethic, but I know I'll be a better friend and person if I do my best not to hurt anyone's feelings on purpose.

My second *law of life* is to not let myself be influenced by what other people think. I have to spend my whole life living with myself, so I want to be comfortable with who I am. I do not want to feel ashamed or guilty. I want to be true to my own self and my own conscience. This idea is not unique. Shakespeare even wrote about it. "This above all: to thine own self be true." Sometimes it's really hard to say or do what I know is right when I know I'll probably get made fun of. In the end, though, I'd rather be called a geek or a wuss than to have to call myself dishonest or cruel. I need to be true to what I know is right. For example, one day this year a kid was making fun of someone else. I told him to shut up and he turned to me and said, "You're really weird. You stick up for other kids but no one sticks up for you." I know he meant to put me down (and it did make me feel bad), but I took his comment as a compliment. I can live with myself if I do what I think is right even if someone else thinks it's weird or wussy.

In conclusion, I want to say that I do not always have the courage to follow my "laws." It's really hard to do! But, I feel really awful when I break them. A few minutes of feeling clever because I made kids laugh at someone else's expense, or a few minutes of feeling cool because I went along with the crowd aren't worth the feelings of disappointment in myself. I want my grandfather and my family to be proud of me. I want to be a good friend. But, most of all, I want to be proud of myself.

William would like to combine his love of travel and flying into a career as a commercial airline pilot. He believes that "Everyone my age should have the opportunity to define what's really important to them. Writing the essay, I learned a lot about myself and what is important in my life."

⌒

FAIRFIELD COUNTRY DAY SCHOOL *LAWS OF LIFE* ESSAY CONTEST

Mrs. Worthington Johnson sponsors the essay contest at the Fairfield Country Day School, an independent day school for boys. Mrs. Johnson first heard about the contest from Sir John Templeton, and she was struck by his vision.

The essay contest is a key component of a course entitled "Inside/Out." The goal of the course is to address "inside" values and "outside" pressures. Since 1996, every Fairfield Country Day sixth grader writes an essay as part of the course, and the school's faculty judge the essays. The cash prizes are awarded at a school-wide ceremony that is held each year in early June. ✳

Nick Maney
age 17

Palm Beach County
Laws of Life Essay Contest

PALM BEACH COUNTY, FLORIDA

on RESPECT
"What I learned from Carl"

M Y MIND seems always to return to the day that I met Carl. The city bus, with its mechanical hiss and its slightly dizzying engine-exhaust fumes, stopped at the corner of 31st and Centennial Drive to pick up the daily commuters, a group in which I was included. Boarding the bus, I looked, seemingly in vain, for a place to sit, because I hated standing in the aisle and being subjected to the rocking of the bus. At last, I spotted a place to sit near the back. The occupant of the seat next to the one I was going for was an older man in a grey suit, well-worn dress shoes, and a black hat like I always pictured reporters wearing, but without the little press card. Sliding into the seat next to the man, I began to read the book I'd been carrying, which was Jack Kerouac's *On the Road*. The man in the seat next to me introduced himself by asking if I'd read any other books like the one I was currently holding, books from the same era. When I told him I had, he seemed to become interested, and, to tell the truth, so did I.

He introduced himself as Carl. He told me about how he used to play the trumpet back in the fifties in jazz clubs. He asked if I like jazz, and I told him that I didn't really listen to it, that I liked punk music. Waiting for Carl to tell me that I should listen to "real music" I was shocked when he just smiled and nodded. He said, "you remind me of myself when I was your age. I remember how my parents hated jazz, how they couldn't see how I could listen to 'that awful noise.' I bet your parents say the same thing, don't they?" Now it was my turn to smile, amused with how right he was.

As the bus ferried us from one side of the city to the other, Carl and I talked about a lot of different things. The more we talked, the more amazed I became at how much the two of us really had in common, despite the age difference. Finally, Carl got off at his stop, and mine was soon after. I haven't seen him since then, but the thought of our connection that day rarely leaves my mind.

Carl really made me think about how much we can learn from each other if we just break through the barriers we've got. I mean, I would have never thought before that day that I could have anything in common with someone so much older than I, just because of age. But Carl taught me that no matter what, we're all just people, and that we should make an extra effort to try and get to know our neighbors and people we see every day, regardless of age, or of race, religion, sex, or anything else. If we all took the time to attempt to understand each other, I think that the world would be a much better place that we could share together, as humans.

Nick plans to attend college and study advertising. During his free time, he enjoys surfing, reading, and playing with his band.

∽

PALM BEACH COUNTY *LAWS OF LIFE* ESSAY CONTEST

Since 1996, over 28,000 young people have participated in the Palm Beach County Essay Contest! Two factors have contributed to the success of the contest: the continued support of local benefactors who believe in the essence of the program; and the enthusiastic involvement of participating high school English teachers who encourage and even gently prod their students to write a *laws of life* essay.

In its first year, the contest was made possible by the combined support of the Palm Beach Roundtable and Northwood University. During the first year, local philanthropist Bren Simon had the opportunity to hear the grand prizewinning student read her *laws of life* essay and immediately pledged to fund the Palm Beach County Contest for the following three years.

In addition to Ms. Simon's support, the Quantum Foundation provides a substantial grant each year to publish the award-winning essays in a paperback book, *Turning Points,* which is widely distributed throughout Palm Beach County.

Since its inception, the essay contest has grown to 21 high schools. This year's awards banquet was held once again at the Kravitz Center in West Palm Beach, where over $17,000 in cash prizes was awarded to the 25 student finalists, and $16,000 in prizes was presented to participating teachers and schools. In addition, Northwood University extended scholarships in the amount of $40,600 to the top prizewinners.

Jack Letvinchuk, Director of Admissions at Northwood University and coordinator of the Palm Beach County Contest, shares why his university supports the contest: "We believe that the contest promotes critical thinking and provides students with a forum to express their core values." ✳

Arliss Feathergill
age 17

Winona *Laws of Life* Essay Contest
WINONA, MINNESOTA

on REDEMPTION
"The epiphany"

I AM NOT PROUD of a lot of the things I will reveal within this essay, nor do I like to talk about them or even dredge up such painful memories. However, if what I write here helps just one person learn from my mistakes, then I would repeat it all once more. This is a story about evil, redemption, and repentance.

I used to be a jerk, one of the biggest in the world. I hated everyone. I didn't care about your race or your religion or your sexuality; all you had to do was be human, and you were a target of my hate. My few friends were ones of convenience; they were the same as I was. Fortunately I had one or two real true friends who stuck by me then and still do; they didn't hate the world like I did. My friends of convenience and I though, we hated everyone—a familiar face or a complete stranger. Our greatest aspiration in life was to get even with the entire human race for what we felt were great offenses committed against us. I was never nice to strangers no matter who they were or how they treated me. My mind was made up to hate the entire world, and I did. I was a sociopath of the worst kind, straight on the path to be the world's next public enemy #1. But that was not the worst— the worst of all this was that I was proud of myself. I was proud of the hate; I was proud of the insanity; I was proud of my psychotic attitude; I was proud of the negative attention I received from everyone. So I continued with this nightmarish life of hate. My heart was made of anger and my vision clouded by rage. For three years this continued, and I sank ever deeper into this pit of intolerance and horrible hate.

On June 11, 1998 my mother and I took a trip out west to visit a successful old friend in Seattle. I had arrived there with the same attitude I'd lived with for the past three years, still one of extreme hate and anger. I still wore my deep scowl even though I was happy to see my good friend Steve after all these years. My mother traveled down the coast, and I stayed with Steve for ten days. I had no idea at the time, but those were going to be the most important ten days of my life. During those ten days, I watched Steve simply live his life. He had friends, money, and a permanent smile on his face. And a small part of me wished I could have that too, but then something happened that changed everything. I remember the exact moment it happened down to the last detail. I was sitting on the porch of his apartment in a rich upper class Seattle suburb. He was calmly smiling and smoking a cigarette, and I was playing with his lighter, still with a dark scowl that was seemingly etched onto my face. I was watching him as he waved to every passing car knowing who was inside and commenting on them as they waved back. Seeing him sit there happy and friendly I suddenly realized...I was an asshole.

This realization took less than one second, but it felt like an eternity. In that one moment my entire life shattered like a falling mirror hitting the ground. Everything I thought, believed in, and acted upon, disappeared, melted like the ice that had frozen my soul into a cold hard piece of hate. In that one second my entire life changed, my finger stopped playing with the lighter and all the sounds around me were completely drowned out by the tumultuous thoughts inside. My body was filled with a searing pain brought on by a horrible shame. In that one second I woke up from the horrible nightmare that I didn't even realize I was living in. My eyes opened, and I realized that I was evil, but maybe, just maybe it wasn't too late to change.

That night when Steve had gone to bed, I was still up, sitting and pondering what had just happened to me earlier. When I looked back on my life before that point, I did something I had not done in three long horrible torturous years...I cried—I cried until my face and hands were saturated with the salty water; I cried until small puddles had formed on the ground at my feet. My body shook with painful convulsions as I shed tears of shame and sadness as I thought of the reprehensible beast I had been. I let the tears come; the feeling of their cool kiss on my cheeks seemed to quench the fire of shame that filled every fiber of my being. I continued to cry until no more tears could come. But I was still filled with shame and a new anger—anger directed not at the world, but at myself. An anger born because of the reprehensible human being I had let myself become. That night I didn't sleep. I sat outside in the cool, calming Seattle rain, and I thought. Just as the sun buried itself in the west, I decided that I too would bury my former self and as the sun rose again in a new day, I would emerge as someone new, someone who led a life of good. That morning I began my journey of redemption.

It has been almost two years since that day, and it has not been an easy road. In the months following that night I spent the time erasing my old life. I threw away material possessions. I destroyed friendships. I slowly erased who I was inside and began starting over from where I once was. Long before I let myself slip into a raging ocean of hate. It was not an easy task, but I removed myself from under the hand of the cruel mistress of hate and have found myself in the soft bosom of the angel of love. Although I still don't believe I am truly as good a person as I could be, I am far better than I was and far better than most people I know. I do not hate anyone, no one at all. There are people whom I do not like; for those people I wish them well, but I wish them distance. I have gone from hating everyone human to accepting everyone human, no matter what his or her race, sexuality, or religion.

I have come to accept and respect anyone who accepts and respects my and other people's rights to our own beliefs. I still sometimes struggle with my ideals and have found myself too often in a situation of hypocrisy, but I am still unswerving from my path of becoming the person I wish to be. I now have friends and a broad smile, which I nearly always keep. I spend a lot of my time trying to make others smile and laugh and am oftentimes successful. However, there is still one thing I do not tolerate, and that is the evil beast of intolerance and the attempt to thrust upon unwilling people your beliefs and ideals. These things anger me; they remind me of myself before I shed the evil trappings of hate that I had so proudly worn, but now look at in shameful disgust. I still harbor shame for what I was and try to stop others from following in my footsteps. The road of redemption and repentance is harsh. But if you find yourself in the situation I was in it is well worth it. However I urge you all to not even begin the journey down the road to evil, because mine is a fate I want no other human being to experience.

Arliss hopes to become an actor or writer. He explains, "I can only hope that by sharing my story, someone, at least one person will learn not to make the same mistake of hate that I did."

WINONA *LAWS OF LIFE* ESSAY CONTEST

William Schuler, a member of the Junto Club of Winona, Minnesota, met Sir John Templeton on a trip to the Far East. The two talked at length about the essay contest, and Mr. Schuler became sold on the value of the contest. He brought the idea to the Junto Club, and the contest was launched in 1996. In 1998, the Winona Golden K Kiwanis Club became a co-sponsor of the contest, with additional support from Merchants National Bank and Knitcraft Corporation.

This past year, 407 students from Winona Senior High School and Cotter Senior High School entered the contest. The 26 prizewinning authors received cash and savings bonds. St. Mary's University of Minnesota also offered a four-year scholarship to the top winners—a significant gesture that honors Winona students for reflecting on and writing about their values. In addition, the *Winona Post* recognized the winning students by prominently featuring their essays in the newspaper. ✳

Peter MacLean
age 16

Learning for Living UK Competition
UNITED KINGDOM

on INTEGRITY
"Keeping your word"

IT WAS A COLD NIGHT and I was breathing heavily as we climbed above the tree line towards the top of the mountain.

When we reached the summit, we sat down and looked towards the canopy of stars that glittered above us. Every star held in place by the laws of nature, each kept on its course by principles that even the greatest mathematician and the most powerful computer could not calculate.

Newton had tried; he had discovered the laws of gravity. Einstein and Schroedinger had tried. Yet still the universe held its secrets; still its laws were not understood.

Yet as we sat there, looking towards the sky we were sure that there were laws that governed the motion of the starry heavens above, as surely as there were laws that governed the action and interaction of atoms and molecules.

I am a Scout. I was at Glen kin, camping with my friends of the 4th Port Glasgow troop. As we made our way back down the mountain I was thinking about what we had seen. Living in town we don't normally see the stars very clearly, but out here in the wilderness of mountains and locks the whole sky seemed ablaze with tiny pricks of light. "The starry heavens above, and the moral order within"(Kant).

I don't know what put these words in my thoughts, but somehow they struck home and my friends and I began to talk about the Scout law and promise, and wondered whether they were like the efforts of physicists to unlock the laws of the universe.

What if the Scout law and promise was an effort to unlock the laws that govern human society? "Put some force here and the effect will be seen over there." In science cause and effect are direct, often predictable. We wondered whether society worked like that: "Act kindly here and the effect will be seen somewhere else."Or even, "Do an unkind thing here and the effect will be seen in suffering somewhere else."

Sometimes ideas float in and out of my mind without leaving any footprint, but this idea wouldn't go away. When I became a Scout I made a promise:

> *On my honour I promise that I will do my best to do my duty to God and to the Queen, to help other people and to keep the Scout Law.*

I remember having thought how important it was to be making a promise that would be the basis of decisions I would make, possibly for the rest of my life.

Not all Scouts have a Queen, but they still promise to fulfill their duty to the nation and to God and to live in obedience to the Scout Law. Sometimes Scouts find the principles hard to keep, but the promise is "to do my best." Even if a Scout fails, if he has done his best he has done enough.

"The starry heavens above and the moral within." Unlike the laws of the universe, this *law of life* lives not in the stars, but in me. I am bound to the promise, because I chose to be. The promise refers to Scout Law and this sets out seven standards by which each Scout is able to judge his success or failure as a Scout. Maybe these also set a standard by which everybody can judge their success or failure as human beings.

A Scout is to be trusted—A Scout is loyal—A Scout is friendly and considerate —A Scout belongs to the worldwide family of Scouts—A Scout has courage in all difficulties—A Scout makes good use of time and is careful of possessions and property—A Scout has self respect and respect for others.

I threw myself around in my sleeping bag, unable to sleep. Still these words went through my mind, *"The starry heavens above and the moral order within."* I got to thinking about the laws in the Bible. The Ten Commandments are respected by Christians, Jews and Muslims as the laws given by God.

It is as if God had done two things: He had placed a knowledge of what is right in the centre of everybody, and then He had given a law that is outside each of us so that we could judge how well we understood what it ought to be like to be completely human, completely in touch with the "moral order within."

Back at home, I flicked through the encyclopedia and found that some Hindus also believed in a God-given law. They call it the Law of Manu, and it shares much of the Ten Commandments, even including a rule "to honour your father and mother so that your days in the land may be long."

My mind again raced back to the hillside and I remembered the Scout promise "to do my duty…"

Peter plans to attend university and then to fly commercial airplanes. He enjoys listening to music, Scouting, and exploring wild places in Scotland and overseas.

LEARNING FOR LIVING UK COMPETITION

Since 1997, the UK program has been coordinated by the Christian Education Movement (CEM), an ecumenical educational charity in the United Kingdom whose core mission is to help children and young people reflect on their faith and learn more about the major world religions. In the United Kingdom, religious education is a required component of the curriculum, and CEM serves as the primary support to religious education teachers throughout the UK.

The competition is held in schools throughout the UK who respond to a notice from CEM or receive information about the contest on the organization's website. Over 2,000 entries were received for last year's contest. Ninety cash prizes, totaling £1,250, were awarded to the winning essayists at a ceremony held at the Royal Society of Arts in London.

Denise Signorelli
age 19

Wayzata Community Foundation
Laws of Life Essay Contest

WAYZATA, MINNESOTA

on LIVING LIFE TO THE FULLEST
"Last day"

I HAVE BEEN TAUGHT many lessons during my lifetime which stand out in my memory. "Nobody's perfect," "practice what you preach," and "don't count your chickens before they're hatched," are just a few. All of these are worthy laws with worthy principles, but I do not believe them to be the most important. I think the most important law to follow is to "live each day as if it is your last."

When I was first given the opportunity to write this paper, my life was different. I was unsure as to which moral stood strongest in my mind and heart. Then, two weeks ago, my uncle died. Actually he was my step-uncle. I did not know him as well as I would have liked to, but it does not matter. Death is a profound thing. It leaves its mark one way or another on everyone. Whether it happens to be an article in the newspaper about the destructive death rate of a killer disease, or a historical account of the Holocaust in our school books, in society today, death seems virtually omnipresent, yet it is taken lightly. It seems as though we have become so accustomed to hearing the horrific accounts of death in society, unless it hits us personally, we are not affected.

My uncle was diagnosed with colon cancer a year and a half ago. It is one of the most common forms of cancer among middle-aged men. Though he lived longer than expected, my uncle was just forty-nine when he died. Even though my cousins and aunt had the year and a half after the initial shock to prepare themselves for what they knew would eventually take over their father and husband, it did not make the actual event any easier to deal with. I do not think all the time in the world would have mattered, because death is a hard concept to face. No one seems to be able to grasp it. As my step-dad said, "Not being able to just pick up the phone and call the person to talk with, laugh with, and ask dumb questions to is the hardest part of all to deal with."

During the days following my uncle's death, I really wanted to talk to my step-dad about it, ask questions, and hear answers. In reality, however, I could not bring it up with him because I did not know how to approach the subject. I was afraid of death. I am afraid. For me it's the prospect of not knowing what will happen to you, and it's scary.

I am not sure what I had expected after our family received the initial shock, but it most certainly was not what I got when we visited a few weeks later. No mention was made of cancer, and things went on as normal. This much I expected. The difference was in my uncle. Actually, maybe it was not so much a difference as something I had not taken the time to notice before. I suppose I expected him to be depressed, seeing as I would probably feel that way if I just learned I was going to die. My uncle, on the other hand, was anything but. Actually, I do not think I remember ever seeing him happier and more joyful toward life than I did that day. In the few hours that we visited their house, I learned volumes. He carried on as he always had except he seemed more thankful to the rest of the world by having more fun and enjoying our company. He did not give me pearls of wisdom or a famous quote to enlighten me. It was all in his new (or previously unnoticed) per-spective of life. He showed me how to truly live each day as if it is your last. He had accepted the cold truth about what would soon happen to his body, the pain he could expect, and the disease that would eventually kill him, but he kept right on living the way he did before. He did not even look for God in his time of need as some do, he knew where to find Him. He just absorbed all the love and caring from his family and friends who surrounded him and let them make his soul and heart stronger.

My uncle, though he did not try, taught me to live each day of your life as if it is your last. He showed me not to go to sleep at night with regrets about things you wanted to do during the day. He taught me not to rest when there is still anger between you and a friend. He showed me how to absorb the love of those around you and to store it in your heart. If you want to have a bad day, you will have one. I know now, the outcome of my life depends solely on my attitude toward it. It will "make or break you," a teacher once told me. Now I try to go through life not merely to get by, but to really live and experience things, because like my uncle, when it is time, I want to go without regrets.

Denise currently attends New York University where she is studying drama. "The Laws of Life *Essay Contest helped me find my voice as a writer," she explains, "but more importantly, it challenged me to look at my life and embrace what is most important."*

⌁

WAYZATA COMMUNITY FOUNDATION *LAWS OF LIFE* **ESSAY CONTEST**
"What is the one *law of life* that you feel we should all live by?" That is the question posed each year to all high school students in the Wayzata, Minnesota school district. And the responses are diverse, creative, and frequently moving.

The Wayzata Community Foundation has sponsored the essay contest for the last four years, with additional support from Anchor Bank and Norwest Bank. All of the student participants receive an award, and the top 16 are given cash prizes, with a grand prize of $1,000. One of the most special aspects of the Wayzata Contest is that the winners are encouraged to contribute part of their prize money to their favorite charity. Giving back to your community—that's what sponsors feel the Wayzata Contest is all about. ✳

Tamara George
age 15

Alvin *Laws of Life* Essay Contest
ALVIN, TEXAS

on FAMILY, HONESTY, AND BELIEVING IN YOURSELF
"What I learned from my family"

As I HAVE GONE through life so far I have found certain laws that I live my life by. As I grow older and wiser I hope my *laws of life* are still the same and expand into many more. My family has influenced me greatly as to what I value.

The most important of my values is my family. They have always been there for me. When I was little my mom quit work to be home with my sister and me; that just shows how much they care. My family has instilled many lessons and habits in me. They have taught me how to be caring, sensitive, and understanding. These three qualities are those which friends and family look for in a good person. My parents also have taught me to be the best person I know I can be. That has made me go very far in life. I only hope that when I'm older and I have started my own family, my kids will value their family as much as I value mine.

My second most important *law of life* is honesty. Like the saying goes, "Honesty is the best policy." I definitely agree with this. People who are honest have more friends and are greatly respected. I have learned through life that honesty is a great way to get to know people. If you lie about who you are or what you did, people don't want to be around you. Your friends will never trust you when you tell the truth if you lie all the time.

I also lead my life by trust. Trust—you can never go wrong with it. In any relationship, whether it be mother-daughter, or boyfriend-girlfriend, it doesn't matter, the number one thing to think about is trust. When you think about trust you think about keeping a secret, but that is not the only thing there is. Trust is when you stand beside your friend when times are good and bad. Friends will never forget it. That is what trust is and that is why it is one of my *laws of life*.

Another *law of life* that I go by is responsibility. Going back to my first value—family—I have a huge responsibility to my family. Not only that, but I have a responsibility to my friends and to everything else I do. Responsibility ties in with all my *laws of life*; I have responsibility to continue to guide my life using these laws.

My final *law of life* is pride. In whatever I do I have pride in it. If people call me names because I wear a supporting pin for what I do, it doesn't matter, because I have pride in the organization. Every person should have pride as one of his or her *laws of life*. Pride is an excellent thing to have. It shows that you care about what you do.

The laws that I now have will be the same ones I use for the rest of my life. These laws I hope to instill into my children as they grow up and need to start down the right path to life.

Tamara hopes to attend Texas A&M and someday open her own pet clinic. She believes that "writing this essay has showed me that no matter what I do in life I will always have my values."

～

ALVIN *LAWS OF LIFE* ESSAY CONTEST

In Alvin, Texas, thanks to the 18 community sponsors who have gotten involved in the essay contest, the more than 900 health students who participate in the contest can win soft drinks, haircuts, pizza, and gift certificates to local stores. In addition, two $500 scholarships are awarded each year to the top two senior class winners. The contest began during the 1997–1998 school year and remains a huge success. Many of the original sponsors continue to support the contest, and new sponsors are added every year.

Contest sponsors include Alvin Bowling Center, Alvin Community Center, Alvin Community College, Alvin Golf & Country Club, Bayou Wildlife Park, CiCi's Pizza, Domino's Pizza, HEB Pantry Foods, Hair Masters, Helen's Flowers, Jewelry by Chas, Lee Oil Co. Inc., McDonald's of Alvin, Pam's Pan Pizza, Pizza Hut, Sonic, Super Warehouse Foods, and Whataburger Restaurant.

Although free pizza and gift certificates certainly encourage students to write a *laws of life* essay, sponsor Don McKaig of CiCi's Pizza underscores the true benefit of the Alvin Contest: "The contest gives young people an opportunity to think of the ways the *laws of life* benefit each and every one of us." ✴

Joanisa Tenreiro
age 11

Naples *Laws of Life* Essay Contest
COLLIER COUNTY, FLORIDA

on KINDNESS
"Go out and do something kind today"

"Stop it!" My brother screeched.
"Aw...are you scared I'm going to tell Momma?" I teased.

I LOOK BACK on that experience and I think that I could have used some kindness. Kindness is important for many different reasons, and it should be used every place you are.

At school you use kindness as an example to others. I use kindness as encouragement. If someone is about to give up on something, I crank up my kindness and I tell him or her not to give up, then I help him or her. Kindness is a source of getting along. Without kindness, you'd have no friends. Your teachers need your kindness, too. They expect you to listen, be careful, and watch. What if I were at PE and I wasn't listening? I would get the PE teacher upset, and that would not be kind of me.

You should use kindness at home, too. Sharing is a great act of kindness. If you share at home, other good things happen. Once I shared one piece of candy with my sister and the next day she shared a bag of popcorn with me. I also take turns out of kindness, which means no fighting. I take turns doing a lot of things, such as doing the dishes, clearing and setting the table, and playing on the computer. All that leads to a nice, happy, quiet house: a perfect place for homework!

Being kind every day helps you out in many ways: at school with friends and teachers, and at home with family. Go out today and do something kind; you know I will, too.

Joanisa would like to thank her teacher, Mrs. Stewart, for respecting and believing in her, because without Mrs. Stewart, she would not have entered the contest. "The Laws of Life *Essay Contest has meant more to me than just awards and praises," Joanisa adds. "It has taught me that you can do more than you think you can; you can't tell until you try."*

~

NAPLES *LAWS OF LIFE* ESSAY CONTEST

The YPO 49'ers of Naples, Florida have sponsored the essay contest since the spring of 1997. The YPO 49'ers are "graduates" of the Young Presidents' Organization, an international forum that brings together presidents and CEOs at the pinnacle of their professional success. The city of Naples also sponsors the contest with funds collected from the confiscation and auction of property seized from convicted drug felons.

The city of Naples and the school district of Collier County have welcomed the contest and have been instrumental in bringing the contest to public and private schools. Participating schools include St. Ann's School, Lake Park Elementary, Sea Gate Elementary, Gulfview Middle School, and Naples High School.

Each spring an awards banquet is held at the Naples Beach Hotel and Golf Club where several hundred guests congratulate the twelve student finalists from four divisions: grades 4–5; grades 6, 7, and 8; grades 9–10; and grades 11–12. Each division has its own grand prizewinner, and this past year's winners were presented with college scholarships. Teachers also receive awards for their participation in the program.

The YPO 49'ers are proud that the city of Naples and the school district continue to support the contest so enthusiastically. ✳

Andrew Wasuwongse
Age 16

Delaware County Christian School
Biblical *Laws of Life* Essay Contest

NEWTOWN SQUARE, PENNSYLVANIA

on HAVING FAITH
"We are here by grace"

AT A WRESTLING MATCH this past season, I went out onto the mat, the whistle blew, and I wrestled. I had a genuine desire to win and to do well, especially since Charlie Dey, one of the captains, had come over to me before the match to give some words of encouragement. However, I lost that match, and walked back off the mat disappointed with myself. I walked over to Charlie and told him, "I'm sorry," because I felt like I had let him down. But he did not simply say to me, "That's okay, do better next time." Instead, he took me aside and said, "Listen, we're here by grace." Even though I had lost, even though I could have done better, he was not angry. He was still there for me, encouraging me like before. He genuinely modeled Christ's love and grace to me, within the context of wrestling. I thought that was admirable. That one line stuck, and definitely continued to encourage me during the season. It continues to encourage me now that the season has ended. I believe one major biblical law of life is grace. Grace is what gets you on God's path of salvation and grace is what keeps you there.

When I was ten, I asked God to come into my life and to be my Savior. Since then God has shown me the purpose of my life is to serve Him. That day of grace and forgiveness has made all the difference in the complete mess my life could have been without God and now He is now continuously shaping me to be more like Him. Don't get me wrong, my life is far from perfect, but because of God's grace I can carry on knowing God continually forgives me and loves me despite what I do. Grace is of utmost importance. It is the first principle a new Christian must understand in order for all the others to follow. For without an understanding of how much God loved me in order to die for me, how could I possibly model Christ's love to others or do anything else in true thankfulness to God? How could I possibly even try to honor my parents or serve others without any bitterness at all without knowing the extent of God's love demonstrated by His son? In order for these other *laws of life* to follow, I had to first understand my predicament: I was an imperfect being and a sinner, and could never be "good enough to make amends for my mistakes." But by His grace God loved me so much that He sent His own son to die for me and pay the price of my sins, which was death. By confessing with my mouth, "Jesus is Lord," and believing in my heart that God raised Him from the dead, I was saved (Romans 10:9–10). With this understanding as a premise, God enables me to show grace, love, and mercy to others. In my life this means loving my parents, which can really be tough at times. God has shown me grace, and though my parents may not always do the right thing, for they are imperfect just as I am, I still must love them and show them grace as God has shown me. This also means that out of my appreciation of God's love and compassion in my life, I now have a desire to show compassion to others and to reach out in love. Because of His grace, I can serve Him by participating in service projects and by worshipping Him with songs of praise. Because of His grace, I can help to further His kingdom by going to London this year on a mission trip with my church. Because of God's grace I am enabled by Him to love the neighbor next door as I love myself. It is only by God's grace that these things are possible. Those who do not know Jesus cannot know love as Christians do. This is not to say I always act in love, nor do I always love others as I love myself. However, such failure and sin on my part lead to the next incredible aspect of God's grace.

The second most incredible aspect of grace is that God's grace does not stop the day one is saved. It is not simply a one-time deal. I have continually seen God shower His grace upon my life, day after day after day. There are many times I am so sinful I disgust myself. I continually fall into sin, and in my sin I shut God out of my mind saying, "I don't care what You have to say, I'll do what I want to do." I fall down time and time again, yet every time He picks me up and takes me back. It is something so amazing I just don't get it. How can someone who is completely holy even look at someone as black with sin as me? In my times of confession, I find myself repeatedly saying how sorry I am and how much I detest what I have done. Then it hits me: I cannot possibly be sorry enough for all I've done, or all I will do. In those moments I have realized the only way I can possibly be forgiven, the only way I can possibly carry on and continue with my life, is by

God's grace. Without His grace I have no hope. I know this to be absolute. I would not be able to live with myself were it not for His grace. Only by the truth stated in 1 John 1:8, that "if we confess our sins, he is faithful and just and will forgive us our sins and purify us from all unrighteousness," am I able to move on after I have fallen. This is not to say I simply give up the fight and live the way I want to since God will forgive me in the end. By all means no! What it does mean is that on those occasions, and there are many, when I do mess up and sin, God is there waiting to take me back in His arms, forgiving me and allowing me to get on with my business of serving Him. Echoing in my mind are the words of the band Audio Adrenaline, "I get down and He lifts me up, I get down and He lifts me up, I get down and He lifts me up, I get down . . . Every time I get down the Lord lifts me up." How true and how great is God's amazing grace!

God, in His grace, provides a way for man to be saved, and God, by His grace, provides a forgiveness to enable him to persevere. Only by understanding God's awe inspiring grace and love through the sacrifice of His son can one truly show grace, love, and mercy to others. Only by grace can one carry on amidst the sin that so easily entraps him. Having experienced such incredible grace, all Christians should be filled with an uncontrollable desire to tell others about what Jesus has done. By doing so, God's love will be spread and His glory will be made known through all the earth.

Andrew's dream is to attend the United States Military Academy. He runs cross country in the fall, wrestles in the winter, and hopes to soon earn the rank of Eagle Scout. "This contest gave me the opportunity to consider and express the law of grace in an essay," Andrew shares. "Doing so helped to solidify this law of life in my being, and it helped me grow in my love and appreciation for it."

DELAWARE COUNTY CHRISTIAN SCHOOL
BIBLICAL *LAWS OF LIFE* ESSAY CONTEST
Dr. and Mrs. Pina Templeton sent their two daughters to "DC" because of the school's high academic standards and its commitment to the spiritual growth of young people. After both daughters graduated, the Templeton family established the essay contest at the school to

encourage future students to reflect upon their own *laws of life*. Launched in 1997, the contest is held annually under the cooperative aegis of the high school Bible and English departments.

Winning students are recognized for their essays at the year-ending Spring Awards Assembly in the presence of the entire high school student body. "The *Laws of Life* Essay Contest is one of Sir John's great visions," explain Dr. and Mrs. Templeton. "We are pleased to have the opportunity to share that vision with Delaware County Christian School." ✳

chelsea Rose
age 16

Academy of the New Church
Laws of Life Essay Contest

BRYN ATHYN, PENNSYLVANIA

on FAMILY
"Don't take a loved one for granted"

N O ONE should ever take a loved one for granted. You may never realize how important he or she is until you have lost one. I know this because it happened to me. Seven years ago I was leading an almost perfect life. I had friends, relatives, and a normal, ordinary family. Little did I know this was going to change in the near future. My family and my second cousin's family were always together, and it just happened that my best friend is in that family. Our families loved each other dearly. If there were any problems, we'd be there for each other. That is, until my best friend's parents had a divorce. Everything went downhill from there. After that, my mother only let me go over to my best friend's dad's house. This seemed strange, but I didn't think anything of it, ignorant eight-year-old that I was. Months went on, and my mother became more and more against my best friend's mother. They had been almost inseparable before. Every week I would hear a new update on how sad my best friend's mother was because of this. I got sick of it. I ended up spending all my days and nights at my best friend's dad's house because I didn't like the way my mother was acting.

Then, on one of my sporadic attempts to sleep at my house, I heard that my mother had gone to the hospital. It didn't bother me then, because she had gone there before for heart attacks, and she had always come back healthy. This time was different. My father came and told my sisters and me that the doctors had found a tumor in the left side of her brain. This explained why she had been acting so strangely. There was probably only a five minute period where I had the feeling that she might die, which made me think of all the times when my teachers had told the class, "Don't take things for granted, because you don't know how much they mean to you until you've lost them." Whatever that meant. I quickly threw that idea away, because I had convinced myself that my mom could not die. It just was not possible.

After that I went on with my everyday life, not worrying, because I knew that the therapy my mother was getting would heal her. I was living a life of denial, but then everything went wrong. The entire right side of my mother's body became paralyzed. We had to get a wheelchair and a hospital bed for her. Her soft, comforting skin became thin and rough. Her face became stern. Her skin, which before had been scented with the weird but soothing aroma of the natural body wash she used, was now dominated by the nauseating medicinal stench of hospitals. Her round, well-formed, beautiful body turned brittle and bony. The worst tragedy of this evil disease was that she became mute. She could not talk or sing. All the nights of my going to sleep with the sound of her unique voice singing, "Old Black Joe," "Amazing Grace," and "Swing Low" were lost. My bright life of optimism and energy was drowned by a brutal wave of dark, deathly fear. It was Hell.

I changed into a selfish, egotistical girl. I lived the only way I thought there was to live, at a time like this. I was convinced that people should have supreme sympathy for me, that they were in my control because my mother was dying, and my life was so much worse than theirs. To be very frank with you, I was stupid. The time I had to spend with my loving mother, I used to hang out with my friends. I even felt self-conscious and embarrassed when we would go out in public. One month before her death, the doctors said that she was going to die very soon. It was then that I realized how self-centered I was being. That day I understood the saying that one should not take things for granted. I had. I had wasted these last months by practically ignoring my mother.

The next month, I was fully devoted to her. On that fateful morning when she passed away, with my sisters and me in her arms, I knew she was now happy. Most people think it will hurt most after the death, but for me, the worst was over. It was worse to see my mother suffer from the disease and the way I was treating her, than to know that she would now become divinely happy.

I used to say my worst fear had happened, so now I could withstand anything. This is true, but it was not her death which was my fear: it was the fear of taking the most beloved person in my life for granted. I was lucky. I noticed what was happening just before it was too late. But it could be different for anyone. So I say again as I have said before, do not take a loved one for granted. You never know or understand how important they are until you lose one. Believe me.

Chelsea hopes to go to college and travel the world. "I just started writing and all these ideas just flowed," she explains. "I put a lot of emotion and thought into the essay."

ACADEMY OF THE NEW CHURCH *LAWS OF LIFE* ESSAY CONTEST
The Academy of the New Church takes as a central focus of its education the spiritual and moral principles found in the theological writings of Emanuel Swedenborg. The Academy's Girls School launched the essay contest in 1997, after hearing about it from church member Joanna Hill. Since then the contest has become a much-anticipated event of the school year. The contest is funded by Theta Alpha, the women's alumnae organization of the Academy.

Each year, the sophomore class participates in the essay contest, and three women from the Academy community judge the essays. The top prizewinners are awarded cash prizes during a ceremony at the end of the school year. ✳

Julie Johnston
age 16

Guideposts for Teens Magazine
Laws of Life Essay Contest

CHESTERTON, INDIANA

on OPTIMISM
"Positive thinking is contagious"

A LAW THAT I LIVE BY every day of my life is the fact that attitude is everything. No matter what situation you find yourself in, your attitude can make all the difference.

When I was born, the doctors noticed something different about me. My limbs were shorter than average, and they determined that I was a dwarf. A few months later, the doctors shocked my parents with the devastating news that I was also severely visually impaired.

I am now 15 years old and I stand 2'9". I have learned over the years that you can overcome any obstacle with three things: help from God the Father, determination, and a positive attitude.

Through the years, I have been told that I would never be able to do certain things. In almost every case, I have proven this wrong. All it took was a positive attitude and determination. A person has to search for ways to overcome obstacles in life. For example, if I want a drink of water and I cannot reach the water dispenser in the refrigerator, I simply ask myself, "Julie, what can you do to get a drink of water independently?" Then, I come to the conclusion that I need to get a stepstool.

There are a lot of people in this world who have minor obstacles in their lives, and instead of looking for ways to climb over them, they simply feel sorry for themselves their whole lives.

Having a positive attitude can also help change daily moods we get ourselves into. If a person is in a negative mood, he or she just needs to turn it around and determine not to feel bad any longer. Pretty soon he or she starts thinking positively instead. This method also works with other people. If you notice someone is in a bad mood, be positive and upbeat around that person, instead of letting that person influence you to begin thinking negatively.

Positive thinking and attitudes are contagious. Last year, I had a wonderful ninth grade English teacher, who was very upbeat and enthusiastic. We were beginning to learn how to diagram sentences. The first day we started diagramming she made the entire class stand up and repeat the phrase: "Diagramming is fun!" until we looked enthusiastic enough to satisfy her. She explained that if you say something a lot, you start to believe it's true. Every day when it was time to diagram, my teacher would stand up in front of the class with an enormous smile on her face, and she appeared to be having the best time of her life. Her attitude took something most kids see as boring and pointless and made it fun and exciting.

Soon I will undergo four major surgeries. I don't know what the future holds for me but I know I will keep a positive attitude to help me get through it. A positive attitude makes all the difference!

Julie plans to attend college and become an elementary school teacher or a writer. She shares that "The prize money gave me a chance to help an orphanage I had heard about and taught me how God provides when we think of others."

⌒

GUIDEPOSTS FOR TEENS MAGAZINE *LAWS OF LIFE* ESSAY CONTEST
Elizabeth Peale Allen, daughter of Norman and Ruth Peale, believes that "By sponsoring the contest in *Guideposts for Teens* magazine, we can help adolescents to think about those eternal truths that will guide their life. In our hectic and materialistic world it is easy, especially for teenagers, to get swept up in the culture of 'having things.' But concentrating on the *laws of life* opens up a whole wide universe of ideas and truths to live by."

The *Guideposts for Teens* Essay Contest was first launched in 1997 and is open to all teenagers ages thirteen to nineteen. Young people are asked to write about their most important rule, or *law of life*, and to state their "law" clearly in one sentence. They also have to explain how their "law" has made their life and the lives of others better. Last year, about 1,000 young people wrote and submitted a *laws of life* essay to the magazine. Each year, the grand prizewinner is awarded $5,000. ✳

Melissa Jackson
age 18

Wyoming *Laws of Life*
STATE OF WYOMING

on NOT JUDGING OTHERS
"Look with your heart, not with your eyes"

EVERY DAY AFTER SCHOOL I drive to a big brick building on the corner of Spruce Street. Inside this building is another world, a world I cannot enter without leaving the bad events of the day at the door. As I climb the metal stairs to the big yellow door, I can hear the busy murmurs and echoing laughter. The atmosphere is noticeably different, and as I open the door, a fresh breath of innocence overwhelms me and I feel eleven years younger. There are about five kids crowded around a table, patiently waiting for their snack and talking about the fun things that they did at school. A little blond boy spots me and sprints to my side, carefully holding his latest Lego recreation of the Eiffel Tower. Two other boys are tossing a football back and forth, gingerly stepping over two little girls who are sprawled out on the floor, tongues out and concentrating on putting together a Mickey puzzle. There are kids of all ages playing together and helping each other with homework.

Suddenly the sound of crying emanates from two children at the far corner of the room. The caretaker rushes to the their side in hopes of solving the problem. After assertive questioning of both parties, she finds out that the conflict is a result of unequally divided crayons. Deep breath for all of us; we forget that the perversions and standards of society have not been acquired by the innocents of the room. Some of the children do not like each other, not because of appearances, but because of the existence of tattle-tales and toy-hogs. They are too young to care about brown hair or blond, basketball or chess club, whose daddy has the best job. They are oblivious to judgment; unconscious of discrimination. It is in this room that the eyes are solely used for discovery of new things and the heart prevails.

Imagine what today's society would be like if the biggest fights we had were over the distribution of crayons. If a group of people could sit down at a table to discuss a business proposal without judging each other based on employee standing or skin-color. If two nations could accept each other as people and get past the contrasting religions. If social groups in a high school could realize that every person is an individual, no less or more important than any other. I think that the number one problem in today's world is that too many humans look with their eyes, not their hearts.

There was a boy who came to our school from Alabama. His way of talking was different; his southern drawl made him seem stupid and unapproachable. Maybe it was his weight, or the way he always wore baggy overalls and stretched out t-shirts, but he was always seen sitting by himself at the lunch table and only a few of the students at the school knew his name. We all felt sorry for him, but none of us would make the first move. Even I walked past his table with my head down and my ears burning because I knew in my heart what I should do but I was so fixed on what I was expected to do. This boy eventually moved again, but his stay at the Rawlins High School was probably the worst experience of his life; he didn't even have a chance the moment he set foot on the engraved tiles in the front lobby. The other day I was talking to one of his former teachers and his name was brought up into our conversation. I found out that he was the sweetest and most compassionate boy and that he was very smart and a really good writer. All these qualities that this boy had possessed and we judged him based on his physical appearances; we looked past his soul to the part of him that would only last as long as he resided on this earth.

Suppose you were given the choice of electing a world leader and you were given three options:

Candidate A associates with crooked politicians, and consults with astrologists. He's had two mistresses. He also chain smokes and drinks eight to ten martinis a day.

Candidate B has been kicked out of office twice, sleeps until noon, used opium in college, and drinks a quart of whisky every evening.

Candidate C is a decorated war hero. He's a vegetarian, doesn't smoke, drinks an occasional beer and hasn't had any extramarital affairs.

You would probably choose Candidate C because he sounds like a much better person than any of the others. This thesis is presumed based on Candidate C's history; it is assumed he is very self-disciplined and reliable. The others seem like they wouldn't take the job seriously and conduct illegal affairs undercover. Before choosing a person most suited for the task, before making a judgment based on appearance, try to learn as much as possible about the person. Candidate A is Franklin Roosevelt, one of the most liked and respected presidents America has ever had. Candidate B is Winston Churchill, who helped America through World War II. Candidate C is Adolph Hitler. It cannot be inferred from the description that he is racist, discriminative, and power hungry, but it is also evident that he possesses some admirable qualities. The true qualities cannot be construed from the other two descriptions, because the two men described had a considerable impact on America. Look with your heart, not with your eyes.

Every day we encounter people, whether it be at work, school, or the grocery store. What would life be like if we were all afraid to crawl out of bed every morning, get dressed, and leave our house because of these people? There is a man in my community who faces this every day. He doesn't know what to expect one day from the next; he goes to work every morning not knowing if he will be scorned or desecrated. But he arrives and releases so much passion toward his profession that it is unimaginable. If he can impact someone and reveal one truth to one person, he can go home feeling he has done his job. Regardless of every quality he has, there is one characteristic that is the basis for the way he is treated. He is homosexual. This fatal "flaw" causes him to be avoided by many who believe that his sexuality signifies his true character, and he is beleaguered by many who believe that he deserves to be punished. I have had a chance to get to know this man, and he has been a big influence in my life; he has been able to provide the inspiration I didn't think was possible. He inspires me just by getting up every morning to face the wretched world. He inspires me by explaining ideas that no one ever had the patience to do, and in the way he has so much faith in my work. I am also inspired and amazed and captured at the way he isn't judgmental of others. He is so forgiving; he doesn't degrade the people who degrade him because he takes time to understand the background of their opinions. He accepts that some people look with only their eyes, and he overlooks this fault that plagues him every day of his life.

Today, it is no longer about the inside of a person. It is about what is on the outside, what is normal or not, what is acceptable. To people it is about race, color, social class, religion, culture, looks, money, reputation, political party, etc. More and more, the first impression is the binding stereotype. We need to realize that we only see the surface of the ocean in making these judgments, and by disturbing the surface, by touching the water, there is a whole new world that was not known to have existed.

"Look with your heart, not with your eyes."

This law is important in my everyday life. There are people in my life who I don't necessary like, but I am able to accept these people by realizing that they have their own side to the story. I don't have any enemies because I try to get past the stereotype and see the good in a person.

Why is my *law of life* important to the new millennium? Because it is the hope that every person can get along in peace. If Eric Harris and Dylan Klebold looked with their hearts and realized that they were killing people with feelings, hopes, and dreams, the Columbine incident would never had taken place. If the Russian troops of Chechnya would have seen the other viewpoint instead of looking only with their eyes, hundreds of rebels would have survived. It is the hope that we can learn that every person has more to them than what is on the outside, and that we can accept that we are equals in a world full of differences. There are always two sides to a situation, two beliefs, always the question of wrong or right, but if we take a moment to see with our hearts, we are more able to understand both viewpoints and accept every person for what he or she truly is.

Melissa plans to attend college and earn a degree in journalism. She believes that writing a laws of life *essay "convinced me that as a teenager, as a high school senior, as a young girl, I have something to say, something worth listening to."*

WYOMING *LAWS OF LIFE*

The idea for the Wyoming Contest was hatched in 1997 after Rhonda Zimmerman heard Sir John Templeton give the keynote address for Casper College's Business Awareness Week. Working closely with the Casper College Business Division, and especially with Glenda Pullen and Gary Donnelley, Ms. Zimmerman brought the contest to all 49 high schools in the State of Wyoming.

The annual awards dinner is held at the Casper Petroleum Club, and Jim Geringer, the Governor of Wyoming, is usually on hand to congratulate the winners. The top statewide grand prize is $2,000. The teacher of the grand prizewinner is awarded $300, and school coordinators also receive a gift for their participation.

The contest is made possible through the financial support of the following individuals, companies, and foundations: Convenience Plus Stores, Bailey School Supplies, Larry and Margo Bean, Foster Friess, the local Coca-Cola distributor, and the Zimmerman Foundation.

"The essay contest brings together the business community and the youth of Wyoming," explains statewide coordinator Rhonda Zimmerman. "As Governor Geringer always says about the contest, 'These are the kids who will be making decisions when I'm old. I want to see what they're thinking.'" ✳

Emily Garrett
age 15

North Carolina *Laws of Life* Essay Contest
STATE OF NORTH CAROLINA

on INTEGRITY
"We must strive to live with integrity"

All else is gone, from those great eyes
*   The soul has fled:*
When faith is lost, when honor dies,
*   The man is dead.*

THIS EXCERPT from John Greenleaf Whittier's poem "Ichabod" enables us to see into Whittier's concept of integrity. I say "concept" because integrity is not tangible, not like a chair or a tree; rather it is in our minds, our souls. I believe that everyone views integrity differently, although the same virtues are usually present.

I think that integrity is one of the most difficult words in the English language to define. The dictionary says that integrity is "firm adherence to a code of especially moral or artistic values." But is that all? Much of what integrity encompasses is not easily put into words; things such as honesty, sincerity, having good motives, and having a standard of morals which one is not willing to compromise and will overcome obstacles to maintain. These things may not sound that complicated, but in reality they are.

For convenience, I have grouped together honesty, sincerity, and having good motives. Often we are faced with a situation in which these traits are put to the test, and we are tempted to compromise these factors of integrity for personal gain. For example, one may cheat on a test to get a good grade, or lie to someone to keep from getting in trouble. Even though one may get temporary gain by being dishonest, the end result is unsatisfactory. Sometimes, we say things without meaning them. If a person says something and you laugh, not because you thought that what they said was truly funny, but to make fun of them, that is being insincere. Or if one says "I'm sorry" or "thank you" but doesn't mean it, then they are being insincere as well. The third trait in this group is having good motives. To me, this means that I shouldn't use people for my own gain. This is difficult because we have a natural inclination to do whatever it takes in order to get what we want. There are several reasons for which we use people. The person whom we take advantage of could have money, or nice clothes to borrow, or a nice house at which to spend the night. Sometimes, it is because of who they are or whom they know that makes us want to be "friends" with that person. This is not ethical, though. If we decide to get acquainted with someone, it should be because we like their personality and sincerely want to get to know them, not because they have "connections" or season tickets to our favorite ball team's games.

Now, I have written about having a standard of strong morals which one is unwilling to compromise, despite obstacles. My grandfather was once faced with a situation that challenged his beliefs when he was pastoring a church in a southern state. The public schools had been integrated for about two or three years prior to the time that this story took place, but the churches were still strictly segregated. My grandfather had come to realize that all people are equal, and was preaching sermons on integrating the church. He was also saying that God was not pleased with Christians being segregated, and he said that if an African American came into the church, they should welcome him into the congregation because that was what God would have them do. One night, though, Granddad received an anonymous phone call threatening that, if he did not quit preaching integration of the churches, the Ku Klux Klan would come to his church. At that time, the KKK was known to burn buildings and to kill people who supported African Americans and believed that they should have equal rights. However, my granddad knew that he could not compromise what God had revealed to him to be right, so he continued to speak against church segregation.

Then, as threatened, one Sunday morning during the church service, some members of the KKK entered, wearing the white robes and peaked caps of the Klan. He ignored them, and kept right on preaching his sermon. After the service they left, and he never had any trouble with them again.

In this example, my grandfather defied what was popular in order to stand up for his beliefs. He did not abandon his integrity because of a threat. When his opponents saw that he refused to compromise, they left him alone.

One may say, "That was a story about a man upholding his concept of integrity, but my concept is not the same." If this is your thinking, perhaps you believe, as Ralph Waldo Emerson wrote, that "nothing is at last sacred but the integrity of your own mind." But is this belief reasonable? For if integrity were simply what everyone believed to be right for themselves, our society would be horrendous! Crime would flourish because anyone might think it was all right to kill everyone or to steal everything they see! We humans tend to think of ourselves as good, but we are actually sinful. That is how we have been born, therefore it is not our natural inclination to be honest, sincere, to have good motives, or to uphold good moral values. Integrity must be something more than simply our minds' ideas.

Then how can anyone have integrity? My answer is that: we cannot do it on our own; the achievement of perfect and complete integrity within our own human ability is impossible. However, in the Bible, we find the only One that can help us. Philippians 4:13 says, "For I can do everything with the help of Christ who gives me the strength I need" (New Living Translation). Although we cannot achieve perfect integrity, Christ can and will help anyone who asks. Rather than conforming to the low standards of those around us, we must strive to live with integrity. For, as Dr. George Washington Carver once said, "When you do the common things of life in an uncommon way, you will command the attention of the world."

Emily plans to attend a four-year college and major in English. She believes that "Writing this essay has been beneficial to the development of my character and has helped me uncover the path for my future."

⌒

NORTH CAROLINA *LAWS OF LIFE* ESSAY CONTEST

The Jesse Helms Center launched the North Carolina Contest in 1997 to reinforce positive character development at the middle and high school level. The Center is an independent, non-partisan, non-profit organization established to promote understanding of the principles of democracy, the free enterprise system, and moral values.

The contest is not administered in a particular school. Rather, it is offered to all interested students throughout the State of North Carolina, who have only to contact the Helms Center to participate. All winners receive U.S. Savings Bonds, and this past year, the first prizewinner in the senior high division won $1,500.

Each year, the North Carolina Contest focuses on a different *law of life*. This past year, students were asked to explore what it means to have personal integrity, and why pursuing integrity is important. In their essays, students often used examples of people they know who model integrity or recounted an experience in which they learned the value of integrity. ✳

Mollie Barnes
age 15

Kiwanis *Laws of Life* Essay Contest
DICKINSON COUNTY, IOWA

on KINDNESS
"The simple hand that I have to offer"

IT WAS SUNDAY AGAIN and I could hear the coins clinking and clanking in the special can that the teacher had to collect money for needy people. I could tell it was getting heavy because the coins made a deeper sound as my classmates generously slid their coins through the slot. I proudly pulled two shiny quarters out of my coin purse and polished them on my skirt. Some of my friends recycled cans for the money that they brought and some took it out of their allowance, but every child brought what they could to help people in need. I was so proud to have fifty cents that week because I usually only brought a quarter. My teacher always told me that even a penny was a *mitzvah* and every little bit helped. As I dropped my coins into the can, I felt that I was doing my part and I smiled.

A mitzvah is like a simple random act of kindness, except there is nothing random about it. When I learned about what a mitzvah was, I was only five, and at that time, I didn't realize the importance it would play in my life. In kindergarten I learned that collecting money to help hungry people is a mitzvah. A mitzvah is an action that a person performs to make our world a kinder, safer, and more humane place to live.

As I have grown older, I have come to understand mitzvahs in a different way. I want to feel that I am doing my part every day, not just on Sunday. My *law of life* has become performing acts of kindness every day. Not only do I want to do mitzvahs, but I want to do them wholeheartedly and with grace. I want to help people without making them feel indebted to me. I have come to realize that mitzvahs are not about solving world problems, mitzvahs are about simple things that

I can do in my life. Simple things like smiling at someone who looks lonely, reaching cereal from the top shelf for an elderly woman in a store, or helping my little sister study cell structures until eleven o'clock at night are examples of mitzvahs. In my life, I want to help people by being a special piece of today's busy, complicated puzzle.

Jewish tradition has stressed the importance of performing mitzvahs. I believe this is because acts of kindness lead to more acts of kindness. Mitzvahs seem to have the ripple effect because when I smile at someone, I often get a smile in return. When I do something kind for someone, they might pass the kindness on.

Although I have been taught the importance of mitzvahs, I have chosen to make kindness a standard of my life. Doing a simple mitzvah every day is not difficult, in fact it has become second nature. These things that I choose to do are not intended to benefit me. While personal recognition and gratification are not the purpose of doing mitzvahs, I am somehow left with a feeling of self worth and enrichment as well.

An important expectation that I have for my life is to control what I do by my actions. I truly believe that doing a simple mitzvah for someone is an amazing way to find my personal identity. Performing mitzvahs allows me to become closer to the person that I strive to be so that I know that I am living to my full potential. I feel connected to who I truly am when I show love and kindness toward other people.

Mitzvahs are an integral part of my religion and more importantly, they are a standard that I have set to live by. Mitzvahs have shaped who I am and how I interact with the people around me. In first grade, I always felt inspired by the way that my mitzvahs affected people around me. Some of the warmest feelings that I have ever felt have come from mitzvahs. These simple acts of kindness have sculpted my heart. At night, when I turn out the light and climb into bed, I need to have a feeling of self respect for who I am and what I do. Without my *law of life*, I would feel empty and alone because to me, a helping hand connects me to a world that needs the simple hand that I have to offer.

Mollie was recently inducted into the National Honor Society and Beta Club. She hopes to become a pediatrician. Mollie shares that when she wrote her essay, "I was living in a small town in Iowa where there were few Jewish people. I felt very vulnerable expressing these personal beliefs. I was excited to see the positive responses of community members as they read my essay. It was easy to recognize our similar values and standards, even with our diverse religious backgrounds."

KIWANIS *LAWS OF LIFE* ESSAY CONTEST

In Spirit Lake, Iowa, two Kiwanis clubs, the Sunrise Kiwanis and the Noon Kiwanis, have come together to organize and promote the essay contest. The Kiwanis clubs heard about the contest from Berkley Bedell, a prominent Spirit Lake businessman, former United States Representative, and friend of Sir John Templeton. The contest started in the spring of 1998, and Eileen Perra has been the contest chairperson since the very beginning. Thanks to Ms. Perra and a group of dedicated volunteers, the contest is fully financed by donations from local businesses and individuals.

All four community high schools in Dickinson County participate in the essay contest: Harris-Lake Park, Okoboji, Spirit Lake, and Terril. In the most recent contest, 35% of all of the students in the county participated! One hundred guests attended a reception held at Emerald Hills Golf Club, and twelve students received cash prizes totaling $2,700.

Greg Stevens, state representative of this northwest Iowa community and English teacher, praises the essay contest: "I have been involved in numerous writing contests. No other contest has such a positive effect on our young people. The real difference is that the students are writing from the heart." ✳

Laia Mitchell
age 19

Florida State University
Laws of Life Essay Contest

LEON COUNTY, FLORIDA

on HELPING OTHERS
"Learning a valuable lesson"

F ROM MY SEAT in the van, the rows of tomato plants looked like neatly laid pick-up-sticks. It was harvest time near Quincy, Florida, picking season for hundreds of migrant workers. With a team of youth, I was ready to spend a week renovating an old church and community center. Yet after that week of labor, my most valuable lesson came not from my own efforts, but from spending time with the church community.

One kind family invited us to come with them to the tomato fields. Early in the morning we rose, dressed in long sleeves for protection, and went to meet the family. They smiled, slowing their routine to be patient with us. I met their daughter, who was almost my age. She and her brother taught me how to pick the best tomatoes, those of good size and color. In the hot sun, they showed us where they kept water, and laughed with us when we took breaks. I realized how much I had in common with the girl, two young people with hopes and dreams, separated only by space and culture. I learned what it is to understand, to be open to new people and ways of life. That Sunday, I met the girl and her brother again. They came to the church bringing tomatoes and fresh watermelon to share. This family, whose life depended on filling baskets with tomatoes, took precious time to share their profits with us, with me. They understood the joy and goodness of life far better than any of us, teenagers from the city. We were the ones who seemed to have everything, yet it was I who had so much to learn. From their warm and open kindness, I saw the beauty of sharing with others. They, who had little, truly understood the value of giving.

I think often of the girl and her family, where they moved, and how they are living. Her family sparked my belief in the necessity of caring, compassionate respect for others. The migrant people showed me that I, one with so much, have a responsibility to share with those who have little. I went to spend a week giving and ended up receiving so much more. I believe that by giving, with honest respect and cooperation, we can truly be part of the human family.

Laia currently attends the University of Florida. She shares that "Writing this essay helped me clarify my thoughts and pinpoint some of my strongest beliefs."

⌒

FLORIDA STATE UNIVERSITY *LAWS OF LIFE* ESSAY CONTEST

Through its Center for Civic Education and Service, Florida State University has helped to sponsor the essay contest in Leon County high schools since 1998. According to President Talbot D'Alemberte, "Florida State University is pleased to join with Leon County schools in sponsoring the essay contest. The *laws of life* essays are shining examples of the intelligence, depth of commitment, and passion of our future leaders."

In 1999, over 1,000 essays were submitted from eight Leon County high schools: Godby, Leon, Lincoln, Maclay, North Florida Christian, Rickars, SAIL, and the Florida State University School.

The awards banquet was held at Florida State University. At the banquet, top finalists were awarded cash prizes totaling more than $3,500 and were recognized in front of an audience of Leon County school officials, university administrators, parents, and members of the press. ✳

Angela Ross
age 13

Gesu *Laws of Life* Essay Contest
PHILADELPHIA, PENNSYLVANIA

on OPTIMISM
"The only person in charge of my attitude is me"

THE *law of life* that appears most important is a positive attitude. A positive attitude will help me overcome the impossible. It can determine whether I will succeed or fail in life. I have witnessed different attitudes of many significant people, showing what a positive attitude can do for you in life. It can move mountains, cross troubled waters and help me reach my dreams.

I am inspired by Ms. Debra Clark, who is a good friend of the family. Ms. Clark is a caseworker, an assistant teacher at Community College of Philadelphia (CCP) in the learning lab, and a Sunday school teacher at the church she attends. With all this to do, she still finds time in her busy schedule to help the elderly with housekeeping, shopping, and attending to their medical needs. Ms. Clark provides childcare for abused women and reads to schoolchildren. When it snows, you will find Ms. Clark outside shoveling snow for her neighbors. When Maya Angelou was writing her poem "Phemonema Woman," she must have been talking about Ms. Clark. I should probably mention that she is visually impaired. Ms. Clark has a positive attitude about everything. She is able to look beyond what she is lacking in sight and help others reach their goals.

What is an attitude? An attitude is a manner of acting, feeling, or thinking that shows one's disposition or opinion. A positive attitude can allow me to achieve goals and accomplish dreams. On the other hand, a negative attitude will get me nowhere in life. I will not be able to achieve or accomplish any of my dreams or goals.

An attitude is very powerful. It can build or destroy a relationship, home, a dream; a person's life. As a young female, I had a very bad attitude. I would always walk around in bad moods. It was something inside of me making me so hostile. I decided to take it out on anybody who came in my way. Most people didn't want to be bothered with me. The ones who did get involved wished they hadn't. My attitude was known as the "virus." It was not contagious, but it was hurting my body and mind, as well as others. It was like a poison I had that needed to be cured.

The first time I met Ms. Clark, she was full of happiness and joy. I couldn't understand why she was happy. Here was a lady who was blind, telling jokes, and laughing in her condition. It was just unbelievable. At that point in my life, I decided I needed a change of ways. If God allowed Ms. Clark to be positive, then I knew the world was not a bad place after all. Besides, I didn't want to be lonely and miserable all my life. For that reason I turned over a new leaf. Every night I pray to God and ask Him to help me with my attitude, so that I can make a positive change in my life as well as others. I am thankful for what I have and am using the talents I have to help others—and I'm not focusing on what I don't have. I realize now that a positive attitude can make a world of difference in my life and the lives I touch.

The only person in charge of my attitude is me. I have chosen to accentuate the positive and eliminate the negative. I have not yet reached the point where Ms. Clark is, but when I get older I want to be just like her. I discovered I always have choices and sometimes it's only a choice of attitude. It's up to me if I want to succeed in life or fail. In my journey of life, I am striving to be the best I can be, with my new positive attitude.

Angela plans to attend college after graduating from high school. She enjoys spending her spare time helping children. "If my writing can change one person's life," Angela believes, "then I have helped someone."

GESU *LAWS OF LIFE* ESSAY CONTEST

The Gesu School is an independently run Catholic school located in a distressed neighborhood in North Philadelphia, a community in which almost two out of three students drop out of public school. The school's 7th and 8th graders have participated in the essay contest since 1997. As they embark upon their teenage years, the contest provides Gesu students with the opportunity to articulate a moral code that will help each one to find success in life.

At the Gesu School, the essay contest is part of a school-wide commitment to student literacy and excellent writing skills. According to school principal Sister Ellen Convey, "The competitive nature of the contest and its tangible rewards motivate pupils to excel on a level above their normal writing assignments."

The essay contest is sponsored by Dr. Pina Templeton, Sir John's daughter-in-law, who explains "The contest is a window into the future and a repository of the past." ✳

Elizabeth Cherry
age 15

Hickory *Laws of Life* Essay Contest
HICKORY, NORTH CAROLINA

on BELIEVING IN YOURSELF
When you look in the mirror, do you like what you see?

ALWAYS BELIEVE IN YOURSELF no matter what; love the person that you are and appreciate what God has given you. These are *laws of life* that are useful for everyone. I think that before people can live happy lives, they must believe in and accept themselves. The hardest thing for individuals to do is to look in the mirror and like what they see. Accepting yourself, being thankful for God's gifts, and believing you can accomplish anything for which you strive is hard for all of us. To live a fulfilling life, you must start with believing in yourself as a person.

I have struggled with believing in myself so many times in my life. Struggling with little tasks such as completing homework or memorizing a piece on the piano, I would get so frustrated. You never realize how much easier your life becomes if you have confidence before you take on a task until you say, "I can do this!" Four or five years ago, I began taking piano lessons. Recital time was approaching, and I had a piece that I needed to memorize. Coming home with a feeling of frustration and poor attitude, I just knew I could not accomplish this task. I sat at my piano and told myself that I would never get it finished. What was supposed to be the memorization of a few lines of music is now a life lesson for me. I did end up finishing the piece, and the recital went smoothly. The important point is, looking back on this time in my life, I can see how important it is to know that you can accomplish anything you want to do if you try your best. Now, when I become frustrated with a piano piece, I never give up and think that I cannot do it. Always beginning with a positive attitude, I sit down and tell myself that I can accomplish my goal if I put my mind to it. I realize that I should have this attitude in everything I do. Never give up, believe that you can accomplish anything in which you put your mind and heart.

Love yourself, and like who you are. It is hard for many people to look in the mirror and like what they see. The media of today gives an image that many want to follow. Girls should be tall and perfectly skinny, and boys should be tall and extremely muscular. As a teenager, I fully understand all of these pressures that are put upon us. Every time I turn on the television or open a magazine, I see tiny, skinny little bodies that I think I should have. I have wasted more time wishing I could be someone else than I have living my life to its fullest. To this day, I would love to have the perfect body, but I must realize that I am as beautiful as any "perfect" girl on the cover of a magazine and that what counts the most is on the inside, not the outside. Teenagers are also faced with making decisions at their young age. Alcohol, drugs, and sex are so common for the average teenager. Although many people would laugh at and make fun of me because I have not indulged in these rebellious actions, I have learned that staying away from distractions makes me feel good about myself. I do not have to drink, do drugs, or have sex to be a popular and likeable person; I can be myself. Learning to love myself for who I am, not what I look like and what I do, has really made my life more pleasant and fulfilling. Everyone deserves happiness. It is vital to learn to appreciate and love yourself.

Appreciate God's bountiful gifts that He gives you. I am blessed with so much when many are without shelter, food, and other necessities of life. As I sit and gripe because I do not anticipate receiving a car when I have my sixteenth birthday, there are children all over the world who would just like to have a meal to eat. Instead of dwelling on the luxuries that you do not have, think of those for which you are so thankful. These days, numerous people are self-involved. They care about no one but themselves. God put us on this earth to love and help one another, and so many of us continue to think about what we want. We could be spending more of our time thanking God for all of the wonderful blessings He has bestowed upon us. Think about the talents that you have, and know that God gave them to you for a reason. If you are a compassionate person, visit those in nursing homes with no family. A person with a beautiful voice should sing in a choir to make people smile. Thank God for all that He gives you, and use your talents to help others.

Always remember to believe in yourself, and challenges will seem easier. Love the person that you are, and don't compare yourself to others; you are your own person. Be thankful for God's gifts, and use your talents wisely. The key actions to a happy and fulfilling life are believing in yourself, loving who you are, and thanking God for what He gives you. If people lived by these *laws of life* as I strive to do, they would be content, productive, and fulfilled individuals.

Elizabeth plans to attend college in North Carolina and study to be a teacher or veterinarian. "Many times adults think that teens do not possess values and morals," she shares. "These essays prove that there are some teens in the U.S. who do."

∽

HICKORY *LAWS OF LIFE* ESSAY CONTEST

In 1987, Frederic Wolfe built an independent and assisted living facility in Hickory, North Carolina. After a long run-up period, Kingston Residence of Hickory started to turn a profit. To show his appreciation, Mr. Wolfe wanted to give something back to the community. Around that time, he attended an event where Sir John Templeton talked about the essay contest. Mr. Wolfe immediately realized the contest would be the perfect program for Hickory.

The Kingston Residence soon "teamed up" with the Hickory Jaycees, and since 1997, the contest has been held in six area high schools. Each year, the awards ceremony takes place at the Kingston Residence. Both Mr. Wolfe and the Jaycees believe they are making a real difference in the lives of young people and have begun to expand the contest to other area schools. ✳

Anitra Raiford
age 12

Florida Education Fund
Laws of Life Essay Contest

STATE OF FLORIDA

on THE IMPORTANCE OF LEARNING, FAITH, AND FAMILY
"Reaching my goals"

THIS ESSAY is about the laws that govern my life. I am ten years old and in the fifth grade. I had to investigate what the word *govern* means. According to Webster's Dictionary, *govern* means to rule by right of authority. Also the word *law* means the principles and regulations established by a government. Some of the laws that govern my life are school, church, and family.

School governs my life by offering guidelines to live my life by. School has authority figures and role models that give advice about life. For example, my teacher tells me to say no to drugs. The consequences to drug use are talked about during class. I don't want the bad effects of drugs to rule my life. Another part of school concerns setting goals and trying to reach the goals. My goals include making the best grades that I can and to learn as much as I can.

Church provides the guidelines for my behavior. Some of the things that church teaches me concern my relationship with God. I tithe at church to honor God's authority. I have also been taught to honor and obey my mother. And one of the most important lessons that I have learned is to love my enemies as I love myself. These guidelines all shape my character into something good.

My family is one of the most important things that shape my life. The love my family gives me helps shape my confidence. My family supports me, loves me, and respects me. One of the ways that my family supports me is to encourage me to do my best in school. The love that my family gives grants me the confidence that

I will need to excel in life. As I learn more about respect, I am sure that I can respect others.

I am sure that there are other factors that help me to govern my life. I cannot list them all. My future years may reveal other important laws that will help guide me through life. At this time, I will enjoy school, church, and family as I find a way to reach my goals.

Anitra hopes to attend Spelman College and perhaps go on to medical school. She believes that "Writing the essay helped me to envision my personal goals better, and the foundation of my essay will help serve as a light source to guide my behavior and actions."

FLORIDA EDUCATION FUND *LAWS OF LIFE* ESSAY CONTEST

The Florida Education Fund (FEF), a non-profit, educational organization, held its first essay contest during the 1997-1998 school year. The program was sponsored by the MetLife Foundation. The goal of FEF is to identify and motivate historically underrepresented elementary and secondary school students to excel both academically and socially.

Through the organization's community-based Centers of Excellence Program, the contest is held at local and regional centers throughout the State of Florida. At the statewide awards ceremony held in Tampa, close to 1,000 students, parents, and volunteers listen to the top finalists as they read their prizewinning essays. ✴

Tara Coughlin
age 17

West Philadelphia Catholic
Laws of Life Essay Contest

PHILADELPHIA, PENNSYLVANIA

on HELPING OTHERS
"I can't forget and I won't ignore"

EVERY DAY is a learning process. Seven months ago I spent three days learning about a problem that has no clear, definite solution. The problem still waits; I have not solved it—yet. I say "yet" because of what those three days taught me. The apparent insolubility of a problem is not a comfortable excuse to give in, but a call for fortitude in the struggle to achieve a solution.

I spent three days in August of 1999 in Philadelphia soup kitchens as part of a community outreach program organized by the Community Service Core. I am not a monument of piety. I was simply bored and looking to even out the score a little. I've never had to struggle for much; I was born into a wonderful family and a relatively secure financial situation. Others were born, and continue to be born, into less than nothing: poverty, drugs, prostitution. They don't deserve destitution any more than I deserve plenitude.

So for three days, I lived with about ten other volunteers in a parish-owned row home in northeast Philadelphia. There was one shower, little hot water, no beds, and no air conditioning. Sparse, but as temporary residence none of us minded much, especially when we witnessed the living conditions of the people we were there to help. During the day we served lunch at different kitchens. At night we split up to canvass downtown Philadelphia and tell the people on the street about shelters offering food and an escape from the heat. We talked to many people; some were grateful, others were angry, many were indifferent, a few were crazy. I listened and before I knew it, my thinking had changed.

I believe in the American Dream; if you work hard and make the most of what you have you can succeed. But how do you make the most of a cocaine addiction that began at age ten when the local dealer first got you hooked? How do you succeed when you're kicked out of your house at age thirteen, picked up by a pimp on the street and forced into prostitution? If you have no family, where do you go after a maiming car accident puts you in the hospital for a month, you lose your job and you're left with bills your insurance doesn't cover? Those are only a few stories I heard during my three days of community service in one small section of my city.

When I decided to volunteer for this program it was not my intention to attempt to find a solution for poverty. I wanted to help some homeless people, feel good about myself, even a little self righteous, and move on, content that I had done my part in the war on poverty. The men, women, and children I spoke to made such detachment impossible. I couldn't make eye contact with these people without thinking: There has got to be a cure. This can't be it. There must be some simple solution that just hasn't occurred to anyone yet. I thought of nothing else. I strove to find the answer that was surely lurking somewhere in the recesses of my mind. The recesses proved barren; I could not solve the problem of poverty in my city after working in it and think about it unflaggingly for three days.

The problem remains. It confronts me every time another homeless person asks me for change on my way home. It's the coins jingling in the Styrofoam cup as I pass. It's the empty hand reaching out to me. It's the cardboard sign held up to my car window. So what do I do? I can't forget and I won't ignore. My own alternative is to hold this problem close, where every opportunity to chip away at it can be fully utilized. I know I will return to the kitchens, for I must keep contact with the concrete reality of poverty if I can ever hope to eradicate it. In the struggle to solve this massive dilemma I may one day come to the revelation that has eluded so many. Until then I have to keep going; in life there is no such thing as a simple solution.

Tara has received the Sarah Reinhart award for determination, enabling her to attend her high school on a partial scholarship. She is grateful for everything her teacher, Sister Ave Armstrong, has done for her. "When deciding upon an issue to write about," she adds, "I chose one that evokes strong feelings in myself, in the hope of causing a similar reaction in those who would read my essay."

WEST PHILADELPHIA CATHOLIC *LAWS OF LIFE* ESSAY CONTEST

The contest at West Philadelphia Catholic High School has become a much anticipated event that has had a significant impact on the entire school community in its three-year history. Over 500 people attended the awards convocation this past spring, and 53 students were awarded cash prizes totaling close to $7,000.

A unique feature of the West Catholic Contest is that all of the English teachers receive an honorarium for their participation in the contest. "Teachers who work in faith-based schools have made a special commitment to young people's personal and spiritual growth," says Sister Mary Bur, school principal. "It is so wonderful that our sponsor rewards our teachers for their significant contributions to the contest."

The West Catholic Contest is sponsored by Dr. Pina Templeton, Sir John's daughter-in-law, because she believes in the benefits of this character education program. "The *Laws of Life* Essay Contest allows us to know what our children are thinking and feeling," shares Dr. Templeton, "and it does so through the power of writing." ✳

D. Michael Reynolds, Jr.
age 18

Faith Christian *Laws of Life* Essay Contest
LITTLE ROCK, ARKANSAS

on OPTIMISM
Accentuate the positive, eliminate the negative!

WHILE SOME PEOPLE are born into loving and caring families, others are born into seemingly impossible environments, but no matter how hard a person's life, I believe there will always be at least one person who will positively influence and encourage them. For me, that person has been my grandmother.

There are many *laws of life* that I could write about because my grandmother (better known as "Mamma") literally and purposefully teaches these laws to me. However, she always ends with, "Son, I can tell you all I know and all I've experienced, but ultimately you are responsible for your choices." Ultimately, we all make our own choices in life—good or bad. Not making a choice is a choice in itself. The law of choice puts one in control, but it also places responsibility on the one making the choice.

We can't blame our heritage, our environment, or others for our lives as young adults. We can change what we do not like about our lives by making better choices.

I guess there must be a law that says you become like those you hang around because when I'm with my mamma, I can see how much we think alike (at least I'd like to think so). We were "visiting" one day when I was about fourteen years old. I had gotten into trouble for something at home (which I'm sure wasn't my fault), and Mamma listened to me talk and talk. After a while, she began to share with me, and I listened. Then to my surprise, I heard myself say something to her that she might have said to me. I said, "You know, Mamma, no matter how a child is disciplined, it will do no good unless the child receives the correction that is in the discipline." She was so pleased to hear the insight that after discussing the aspects of what I had discovered on my own, I allowed her to "brag" on me a while. I think she uses the law of "accentuate the positive, eliminate the negative" or as the Bible says in Numbers 14, "what you see is what you get." I hope that that's a true law because my mamma sure says wonderful things about me—to me.

When I'm feeling hopeless or feeling completely frustrated, I hear Mamma's words: "Son, you're not whipped until you're whipped inside," and "nothing is hopeless—there's always an answer.... If you look for it, you'll find it inside yourself." These laws simply say, "Get up and get going!"

Now, most of us teenagers prefer answers to life's problems in the form of a financially generous person. We don't always want to use our minds to solve our problems, but when we do, we find a very important and wonderful law that says, "Youth is for living and learning to make tomorrow's world a better place."

I want to live and learn well.

Mike hopes to own his own business someday. He feels that his teacher, Sister Cook, is a great friend and mentor. "When I first began writing for the essay contest I wanted to relay a message that everyone could understand and relate to," he shares. "I made the decision to write about choices, because choices have an influence on everything."

⌐

FAITH CHRISTIAN *LAWS OF LIFE* ESSAY CONTEST

Several years ago, the assistant principal at Faith Christian asked Principal Joe Irby how the school might be able to help students secure scholarship funds for college. Mr. Irby immediately thought of the essay contest his father launched in Mississippi that encourages young people to write about their values.

Joe Irby realized the contest would be a welcome addition to his school as well as an opportunity for students to earn money for college. With financial support from his father, the Faith Christian Essay Contest was launched in the spring of 1998.

Each year, the awards banquet is held at the Chenal Country Club. Last year, twenty students received scholarship funds totaling over $6,000. ✳

Alexandra Silverman
age 18

Clayton Rotary *Laws of Life* Essay Contest
CLAYTON, MISSOURI

on LOVE
"Don't let the chain of love end with you"

O K, I CONFESS: I'm a country music lover. Some people say country-western music is too twangy, or sappy, and some *is* considerably farmer-ish (although great for line dancing!). But innumerable songs illustrate traditional, altruistic values. And I embrace the principles the music characterizes. Country-western ballads tell heartfelt tales, and no other music evokes my tears on such a regular basis.

Clay Walker's "The Chain of Love" is a flawless example of why my heart belongs to country. The song perfectly captures my feelings about how people should treat each other. The first verse describes a woman in a Mercedes who gets a flat on a rural highway. She watches a hundred cars pass until a man in a "beat-up Pontiac" stops to help her. When she asks what she owes him, he sings the refrain:

> You don't owe me a thang;
> I've been there too.
> Someone once helped me out
> Just the way I'm helping you.
> If you really want to pay me back,
> Here's what you do:
> Don't let the chain of love
> End with you.

A few miles down the road, the woman stops at a small café. She notices the hard-working, smiling waitress is very pregnant and "dead on her feet." So, while the waitress gets change from the hundred-dollar bill the woman gave her to pay for her small meal, the woman slips out the door. Tears fill the waitress's eyes as she reads the note the woman left on a napkin, "You don't owe me a thang…" And it turns out that the waitress is married to the man who helped the woman change her tire at the beginning.

Such musical anecdotes make me want to do for the world what the singers are trying to accomplish with their lyrics. While the songs pass through the speakers into my ears, I engrave them in my mind. Martina McBride's "Love's the Only House" is another example of a country song that inspires us to be considerate of others. McBride sings "…here I am in my clean white shirt with a little money in my pocket and a nice warm home." The description reminds me of myself. McBride recognizes her good fortune and she wants to share it; she wants to invite everyone into her "House of Love." But she knows she can't solve everyone's problems, so she spreads her love in the ways she can. She recounts several of her inspiring stories within the song; one particularly touched me:

> Senorita can't quit cryin'
> Baby's due now any day
> Don Juan got sick of tryin'
> No one there to show him the way
>
> She came down to the grocery story
> 'n' she said
> "I, I wanna buy a little carton o milk
> But I don't have any money."
> I said, "hey – I'll cover ya honey.
> 'Cause the pain's gotta go somewhere.
> Yeah, the pain's gotta go someplace.
> So, Come on down to my house.

A few weeks after I heard "Love's the Only House," my mom sent me shopping. At the deli counter, I saw an old woman in worn clothing carrying her belongings in a grocery bag. She ordered half a pound of chicken salad. When the woman behind the counter handed back her order, the old woman exclaimed, "Oh no! No, this costs too much." And I thought, "I have a few extra dollars in my wallet." So I handed her the money and she thanked me. All I said was, "you're welcome," and then I walked away. At that moment, I understood Martina McBride's wanting to invite everyone in. When Martina McBride and Clay Walker sing about spreading their love, they present the effect of their deeds by relaying the reactions of the people they reach.

I like to keep Martina McBride's "House of Love" and Clay Walker's "Chain of Love" in my mind. Their stories make me realize how fortunate I am, and they make me realize I should share the gifts I am blessed with. I can continue the "Chain of Love" by doing anything from community service to helping my little sister with her homework to giving my best friend a hug. I believe that each small act of love will make the world a bit better, even if it is only to lighten one person's day. Not only do country music lyrics give me *hope* for love and fulfillment in my future, they also inspire me to be *active* in making other people's lives, and my own life, just plain happier.

Alexandra is a member of the National Honor Society and plans to attend Northwestern University. She adds that "During my senior year in high school, I decided that I wanted to share my own laws of life *and possibly have an opportunity to move someone, as past essay writers have moved me."*

CLAYTON ROTARY *LAWS OF LIFE* ESSAY CONTEST

One of the strongest supporters of the essay contest is Sandy McDonnell, Chairman Emeritus of McDonnell Douglas Corporation and member of the Clayton, Missouri Rotary Club. Since 1998, the Clayton Rotary Club has sponsored the contest in collaboration with the School District of Clayton. The awards ceremony serves as one of the Rotary's luncheon programs, and each year Rotary members comment on how much they look forward to the event.

The first-place winners in each category read their essays aloud to an audience of Rotarians, proud parents, and teachers. "The Clayton Rotary is a very proud sponsor of the contest," says Kathy Holman, Clayton Rotary President. "Each year we are astounded by the quality of our young people's submissions and the depth of their thinking. We leave the luncheon having great faith in the youth of today." ✳

Melissa Young
age 18

Optimist Club *Laws of Life* Essay Contest
GEORGETOWN, ONTARIO (CANADA)

on LOVE
"Gone, yet not forgotten"

As I sat down to put pen to paper, many ideas rushed through my mind. There are so many events and individuals that shaped the person I am today. Which one do I choose? After much deliberation, I decided to write about my dad who passed away last year. I thought and thought about two *laws of life* that he abided by. Thinking about him in this way made me realize how much he changed my life.

My dad was born into an alcoholic family. Despite his awareness of the problems caused by alcohol, the disease eventually took its toll on him. It was very difficult for me to see my father lost in a world of turmoil. He affected every aspect of my life from young child to teenager. So many times I sat at his side as he fought for his life in the hospital. He was definitely a fighter, but you can only fight for so long. When he died my life changed so much. How could a father be taken from his family?

From the day he died until now I've tried to put him on a pedestal. I felt I needed to forget the pain he caused me. I wanted to ease the loss by believing he had been perfect. Sitting down and writing my thoughts made me realize I didn't necessarily admire him, I just loved him. I finally allowed myself to understand that what I was feeling was understandable. I no longer had to mask the problems that had formed between us during his short life. I realized I could just love him, not for the person I wanted him to be but for the father he was. I can now look at the past and remember the good times, but I no longer have to shut out the bad ones.

The struggles that my family faced forced me to learn how to cope with problems. My dad left me to ponder what life is really about. He taught me how to survive in an oftentimes cruel world. Somehow he left me with the strength that he never had.

I will always be grateful to him for making me such a strong individual. He was my dad and I have always loved him with all my heart. Even though he has been gone from my life for over a year, I'm just realizing what he gave to me. I understand that he was only human, as am I. Despite the flaws that he had, he taught me that inner strength comes with the knowledge that understanding and caring are the unconditional qualities of love.

Melissa plans to attend a university and study criminology. "It's been a great experience sharing my thoughts with others," she explains, "and I hope that my essay may inspire and comfort others who have experienced similar losses."

OPTIMIST CLUB *LAWS OF LIFE* ESSAY CONTEST

If you live in Georgetown, Ontario, chances are you have come across a booklet featuring award-winning essays on the *laws of life,* published by the Optimist Club of Georgetown and widely distributed throughout the community.

The essay contest is open to all Acton and Georgetown district high school students. The awards ceremony is held at Georgetown Optimist Hall and is attended by the student winners and their guests, along with the mayor and other dignitaries from the community. Every student who submits an essay receives a participation certificate, and the top six prizewinners are awarded cash prizes.

Since its inception in 1998, the essay contest has been coordinated by the Optimist Club and sponsored by Maple Lodge Farms. ✳

Sherrie Crouch
age 19

Kingston Springs
Laws of Life Essay Contest

KINGSTON SPRINGS, TENNESSEE

on COMPASSION AND THE PURSUIT OF EXCELLENCE

"Having a set of rules to live by is a great tool for success"

THE *laws of life* are a set of guidelines that individuals try to follow throughout their lives. The laws that each person lives by are often determined by the way they were taught as a child. As people grow older, however, they begin to branch away from the guidelines of their parents and start to conceive their own laws. As a young adult, I feel as though I have begun my separation from my parents and have started developing my own beliefs. There are several laws that I live by, but the three most important are receptiveness, compassion, and the pursuit of excellence.

One of the most important rules I try to live by is being receptive. By this I mean not being judgmental. I think every person should have a chance to prove him/herself before being criticized and judged. I also believe in giving people more than one chance. Everybody makes mistakes; we should be allowed to make up for them. A problem this world faces is that people make decisions by listening to what everyone else has to say about someone. If we would actually take time to get to know someone we might find that that person is completely different from what we thought.

"Be kind, for everyone you meet is fighting a harder battle." Another guideline I live by is being compassionate, which goes hand in hand with being receptive. Being compassionate includes being kind to others, showing love and affection, treating others with respect, and just being honest. All these factors can make or break any relationship, whether it be among friends, parents and children, lovers, or husband and wife. Leaving out just one of these guidelines could wreak havoc on the best of relationships. Getting upset or saying something hurtful will not ruin the relationship, but if a relationship becomes a constant apology session it is destined to fail. If I follow the Golden Rule, "Treat others as you would want them to treat you," I should not have a problem being compassionate.

The final rule I live by is the pursuit of excellence. Pursuing excellence is a difficult task. Each day I have to find the courage to face the many challenges the day will bring. "Courage is not defined by those who fought and fell, but by those who fought, fell, and rose again." I believe in being responsible for every decision and action that I make along the path to success. Sometimes I make mistakes and bad decisions, but I am able to overcome them by striving to do better the next day. Some people have to learn from their own mistakes while others learn from the mistakes of others. The most important factor in the pursuit of excellence is perseverance. "When the going gets tough, the tough get going." When my world is coming unwound, I give everything a little extra effort. "Never let your head or your heart drop for that is when hope is lost."

Throughout my life I have had to make many decisions, some with the help of others and some completely on my own. My decisions probably would not have been the same if I did not have guidelines to live by. When I make a decision I do not base it on what others will think of me. I make my decision based on whether or not it will conform to my *laws of life*. Having a set of rules to live by is a great tool for success. However if you find yourself following guidelines and consequently feeling miserable and dissatisfied, then take a look inside yourself. You may find you are following someone else's *laws of life*. After all, it's your life; you should be following your own.

Sherrie hopes to attend medical school. As she explains, "Writing a laws of life *essay gave me the opportunity to actually sit down and think about what my standards truly are."*

⌒

KINGSTON SPRINGS *LAWS OF LIFE* ESSAY CONTEST
Prizewinners in the Kingston Springs Contest are honored by having their photo and essay featured in the local press. The contest began in the fall of 1998 at Harpeth High School with the support of the Center for Youth Issues.

One of the unique features of the Kingston Springs Contest is that once English teachers choose the top 12 essays, local principals serve as judges and select the three grand prize-winners. The winners are announced during a live newscast at Harpeth High School, at which students are awarded prizes totaling $1,000.

Now in its third year, the Kingston Springs Contest continues to be a great success! ✺

Paulina Klinkosz
age 13

Mayfield *Laws of Life* Essay Contest
MAYFIELD, OHIO

on HONESTY
"Honesty will help me achieve my goals"

THERE ARE MANY PRINCIPLES and values all people live by. These values help them with dealing with everyday matters. Whether it is to keep their faith at all times or just respect everyone else the way they want others to respect them, it changes their lifestyle. The one law that I live by is honesty. I have always been taught that lying will just get me into more trouble than I might already be in. I have always tried my best at going without lying. Being honest is a quality all people need to have and use to go far in life.

Ever since I was a little kid, my parents have taught me to be honest because it is the right thing to do. As I got older, I realized something very important that could change the way people take me to be as a person. If just once you stop being honest and tell a lie it will dramatically change people's point of view of you and their whole way of acting toward you. When you tell a lie you lose that person's trust forever or have to work your whole life getting it back. You also are going to be taken more lightly on whatever you may say.

It is my personal goal to achieve great things in life and honesty will sure help me get there. For me right now losing somebody's trust would be a truly horrible thing to do. My parents would be stricter on the things they let me do and the places that they used to let me go to. My friends would never again tell me a secret or believe many things I told them. Other people would just keep me as an acquaintance instead of a friend.

Whatever you do for a living or wherever you live, honesty is something important for all of us. Honesty gets you much higher in life than getting into more problems like lying would. Lying can even get you into problems dealing with the government. I can already tell that the great and astonishing people I have met so far are all extremely honest people. Being dishonest to me in a way is like taking drugs. It will permanently reflect upon you and change everything about you. Not only that, but once you lie once you think it won't hurt you to do it again, until you finally have to realize what it's doing to you.

I hope that I'll never fall into a situation where I'll lie. Honesty is just as important to me as my family. Already, I know it is something that will improve my future and my relationship with all people. It is something about myself that I hope to never lose no matter what happens. Most of all honesty will help me no matter if I'm at school, home or just hanging out with friends. It is something that I hope my children will also have and appreciate.

Paulina enjoys swimming and has won numerous swimming medals. "Writing and participating in the Laws of Life *Essay Contest has meant sharing with others what I think is important and necessary in life." She adds, "It also gave me a chance to challenge my writing abilities."*

MAYFIELD *LAWS OF LIFE* ESSAY CONTEST

In Mayfield, Ohio, the Peer Mediation Group and the Teen Institute co-champion the essay contest, which was launched in the fall of 1998. The contest is supported by the Center for Youth Issues and a grant from the Honeywell Corporation.

At the awards ceremony, finalists receive cash prizes, and every entrant is eligible to participate in a raffle—as a way of recognizing that all students who write a *laws of life* essay are winners.

According to Cynthia Rowan, contest coordinator and guidance counselor at Mayfield High School, "We believe that the contest encourages students to take a stand." ✳

Suzanne Schumann
age 19

Hixson High School
Laws of Life Essay Contest

HIXSON, TENNESSEE

on LOVE, JUSTICE, AND COMPASSION
"Principles for true freedom"

IT HAS BEEN SAID that there is no freedom apart from the law. At first, this state-ment may appear contradictory. Many people have adopted the view that no one is free unless he is free to do whatever he *feels* is right in his own eyes. After study-ing the prospect of all men doing whatever they *feel* is right, it becomes clear that it is necessary for there to be certain principles, standards, or *laws of life*. These laws would help ensure true freedom.

I use the Bible as my own standard. The Bible's main message is, of course, of God's plan of salvation through Jesus Christ. That truth is very important to me. In forming my own standards, I look to the "author and finisher of our faith: who was the perfect God/man." Jesus showed in His life the traits that I try to incor-porate into my own life: love, equality, justice, sacrifice, and mercy.

Love and equality go hand in hand. The kind of love that I am referring to is an all-accepting love. It is not based on a person's background, abilities, or appear-ance. Love accepts a person just as he or she is. When I accept people as they are, I view them as equals, not above or below me. Picture these two qualities at work in a community. The richest man is not given more rights or more privileges than the poorest orphan or widow. Both are accepted, neither scorned because of their station in life.

A second and extremely important principle I try to live by is justice. When I'm involved in the middle of a conflict (in the position of arbitrator), I try to be impartial and fair. The role of justice is paramount in a society. It encompasses all written laws. If someone commits a wrong against someone else, it is essential that punishment be meted out justly, neither too harshly nor too leniently. Without justice, the world would be a free-for-all, everyone doing whatever he or she chooses, unmindful of any consequences resulting from their unlawful actions.

The third group of characteristics I would like to incorporate into my life is that of mercy, sacrifice, and serving. I certainly don't hear too much about those traits anymore. Today's emphasis seems to be more on making sure we receive what we deserve. What about those who have even less than what we have now? I know I'm not guiltless when it comes to that. I would like to become less selfish and more giving to those who are in need. If all people devoted even a little portion of their time to helping or serving others less fortunate than themselves, think of what a big difference it would make! What an awesome and humbling experience it would be to see someone quite affluent actually working (not just for show) with the poor and caring for them!

When these *laws of life* (and others like them) are put into practice, they produce order in a society. Without laws and clearly defined guidelines, anything is permissible, and chaos can result. With clearly defined laws and principles, however, an environment where a society can experience true freedom is created.

Suzanne has received an academic scholarship to Berry College in Rome, Georgia. "I found writing the essay quite challenging," she shares. "It forced me to pause in the midst of a busy senior year and really ponder what it was that I most valued."

⤔

HIXSON HIGH SCHOOL *LAWS OF LIFE* ESSAY CONTEST

Hixson High School's commitment to character education is reflected in the pages of *Wildcat Soup*, an award-winning publication that features the views and beliefs of its student writers. Recognizing that the essay contest encourages students to reflect on their core values, the school's prizewinning *laws of life* essays are featured in the publication.

The Hixson Essay Contest was launched in 1998 with the support of the Center for Youth Issues. This past year, more than 500 students participated in the contest, and three winners were recognized at each grade level. Prizes were awarded at a dinner attended by the school board chairman and the local state senator. ✶

Amanda Edwards
age 16

Cincinnati Hills Christian Academy
Laws of Life Essay Contest
CINCINNATI, OHIO

on COMPASSION
"Judge not lest ye be judged"

THE DAY HAD BEEN HOT AND DRY, but it was a cool evening that greeted the inmates as they drove onto our worksite. The crickets were chirping noisily, and I could hear the parched summer grass crunching under their feet as they made their way across the yard. A cool breeze drifted by, chilling me in my tank top and shorts, so that I went to grab my sweater out of the van.

The cool evening was a relief from the sweltering days of summer in Greenbrier, West Virginia. My light sweater was just warm enough, and comforting. I had been working on a Habitat for Humanity house for the past five days under the burning afternoon sun. On this day, though, our group had taken an afternoon trip to a Cold War bunker made for the president because of threats of nuclear war. We normally worked from 8:00 am to 12:00 pm, and 2:00 pm to 6:00 pm. Instead, we worked from 8:00 am to 12:00 pm, and were returning to work the evening shift from 5:00 pm to 9:00 pm. This time happened to be the period that a group of female inmates normally worked. Because we worked different hours, we had never encountered the women before.

My friends and I watched them disdainfully as they disembarked from their guarded van and lit up their cigarettes. I coughed on some sawdust as we began to talk about the ladies. We continued to work quietly on the inside of the house. We knew that someone was working outside of the house on the other side of the wall from us, but had no idea who it was. I had just finished hammering in a nail in record time when we heard someone calling to us.

"Hey, you there," we heard her smoke-laden voice with a New York accent, "could you come out here and give me a hand? I've never been good with hammers." She laughed huskily. We joined in daintily as we peered around the corner. Stephanie and I stepped outside and noticed, to our surprise, that our friend Caitlin was already talking to the woman. They were having a totally normal conversation! I wriggled my toes around in my shoe as I nervously introduced myself to the woman. I found out that her name was Lisa.

The time passed quickly once we began to help Lisa. We taught her how to hold the hammer correctly, walked her around the worksite, showed her where everything was, and, most importantly, introduced her to all our friends. She became more and more friendly as well, introducing us to her friends. The sun began to sink into the velvet folds of night as we got to know her better. When we asked, she even put out her cigarette:

"I've been trying to lose Mr. Ciggy for a while now, anyway."

It soon became clear to us that she wasn't a classic Disney villain, out to get the good guys. It turns out that she was just someone like us, who tended to land the hammer on her thumb more than anywhere else.

The lesson really hit home with me when we said goodbye. It was in the full black of night by this time. A mosquito buzzed by my ear and into the headlights of the school van that was waiting for me. As Lisa was leaving, she said something deeply important, though seemingly insignificant. With so much feeling that I could almost see tears in her eyes, she said, "Thank you."

Lisa and her friends got into the van and it drove away. I watched the van until it turned the corner and drove out of my sight.

My friends and I walked away feeling rather sobered. During the bumpy ride back in the school van that smelled like sweaty socks I contemplated the day. I could see that Lisa's words were more than just a flippant thanks. She was thanking us for treating her like the real person that she was, instead of like an escaped convict from an action movie. Although I felt guilty for laughing at her at first, I was proud of myself for having taken a step forward. It seemed ironic that I thought it would take hard work at Habitat for Humanity to teach me about giving; yet all it took was a brief encounter with one ordinary woman. God's law says, "Judge not lest ye be judged." I learned a great deal about this law that night in West Virginia. Seeing someone through the eyes of kindness instead of condemnation opened my heart to the truth that we are all loved by God. This lesson continues to help me become the kind of person that I need to be if I profess to be a

Christian. After all, who wants to follow a man whose followers reject those most in need of His compassion?

Amanda recently won an award for her commitment to community service. She hopes to continue her mission work, perhaps serving as a volunteer for Habitat for Humanity.

CINCINNATI HILLS CHRISTIAN ACADEMY *LAWS OF LIFE* ESSAY CONTEST

Many of us remember special gifts our grandparents have given us over the years. Mr. and Mrs. John Davies, whose five grandchildren attended Cincinnati Hills Christian Academy, have given a very special gift to their grandchildren's school. Realizing the value of the essay contest, they have sponsored the program at CHCA for the past three years.

Each year at the Academy, middle and high school students are invited to write a *laws of life* essay, and a local panel of distinguished judges selects the top prizewinners. For this past year's contest, the John and Shirley Davies Foundation donated prize money in the amount of $20,000!

"I believe the solution to the problems of the world lies in education and communication," says John Davies. "The *Laws of Life* Essay Contest is a venture in both. What impresses me most about the contest is that the kids have to write their essays on their own—without parental influence or involvement." ✳

Tyler Brinkmann
age 14

Carlyle Junior High School
Laws of Life Essay Contest

CARLYLE, ILLINOIS

on TRYING YOUR HARDEST
"Success is a journey, not a destination"

IT IS VERY IMPORTANT to have a *law of life* to base your life on. A *law of life* that means a lot to me is: Success is a journey, not a destination. It means that what matters is not necessarily where you are at the end, but what you accomplish while you are trying along the way. It means that no matter what, as long as you try, you can never fail. It means you can learn from your mistakes and continue on the next journey a little wiser.

One person I believe that shares my *law of life* is Mark McGwire. He didn't get caught up in the home-run chase in the 1998 season, but instead played every game in the best way he could. And, most of the time, he helped his team. He didn't just go out there and hit home runs because he wanted to be ahead in the end, but because he wanted to make it a good season for his teammates and him.

I also think the 1999–2000 St. Louis Rams as a whole are utilizing my *law of life*. They play every game with their full potential instead of letting a few winning games go to their heads. They stay focused on playing in the Super Bowl. They know that even if they don't go all the way, they still will be successful because they have had a good journey. Even though they lost some games, they didn't give up.

It does not matter if you do not have the ability to be on top in the end, to win the championship; all that matters is that you worked hard the whole time. There are a few people in the world who already understand what it means. They understand that success is a journey, not a destination. But wouldn't it be a much better world if everyone did, if everyone would realize that someone will win and someone will lose, but what's important is that both sides need to try their best? After all, it's not who wins or loses, but how well you play the game, and I hope I have applied this in my own life.

Tyler enjoys helping his father on the farm and riding his four-wheeler. He was co-valedictorian of his eighth-grade class and looks forward to attending college.

CARLYLE JUNIOR HIGH SCHOOL *LAWS OF LIFE* ESSAY CONTEST
This is how Agnes Becker, language arts teacher at Carlyle Junior High, describes the essay contest: "Finally, a contest that honors students for having a moral conscience!" She adds, "Students are often honored for their physical abilities or attributes. This contest challenges them to look into themselves, decide what's important in their lives, and share it through an essay." Ms. Becker, who coordinates the essay contest at Carlyle Junior High, believes that the contest helps her school to promote positive character traits.

With the support of the Center for Youth Issues, the Carlyle Junior High School Yearbook, and Peer Helpers, the first contest was held in the fall of 1998. The contest continues to be very popular among students and is strongly endorsed by community organizations and the local chamber of commerce. Local businesses, such as Hardee's, donate meal and gift coupons to all of the students who write a *laws of life* essay, and the top winners receive cash prizes. "Although the money and prizes are nice," says Ms. Becker, "the participants most enjoy receiving the recognition they get from the community." ✳

Wu Meng (Wendy Wu)
age 17

The I*EARN *Laws of Life* Essay Project
CHINA

on LIVING LIFE TO THE FULLEST
"Enjoy every second"

If there is light in the soul,
There will be beauty in the person.
If there is beauty in the person,
There will be harmony in the house.
If there is harmony in the house,
There will be order in the nation.
If there is order in the nation,
There will be love all over the world.

LOVE, THE ONE CREATIVE FORCE. We all long for it. But unfortunately, when we have love, when our life is full of love, we usually don't feel it is very precious. We don't value it, until we lose it.

When I was in junior middle school, I was always unsatisfied with my life, for it was too monotonous. Studying, eating, sleeping. We did the same things. Nothing was special. But when I went to senior school, everything was completely changed. I began to miss my old class, my old classmates. All of the memories came clearly back to me. Although there were no great pleasures, a great deal of the little ones did make me happy. Although life was deadly simple, it was filled with joy and love. However, the most terrible thing was that I never realized that I was happy. I was so accustomed to the feeling that my senses were deadened to it. When I finally realized it, all the good times had already gone. Now, I've learned

I should live in the present world. Not to be forever regretting the past, or antici-pating the future, but to get the most that you can out of every instant. It's like farming. You can have extensive farming and intensive farming. Well, I am going to have intensive living after this. I'm going to enjoy every second, and I'm going to know I'm enjoying every second, and I'm going to know I'm enjoying it when I'm enjoying it.

Most people don't live; they just race. They are trying to reach some goal far away on the horizon, and in the heat of the going they get so breathless that they lose all sight of the beautiful, tranquil country they are passing through; and then the first thing they know, they are old and worn out, and it doesn't make any dif-ference whether they've reached the goal or not. I've decided to sit down along the way and pile up a lot of little happiness. Enjoy every second, the true secret of happiness. Enjoy every second and suffering disappears and love remains. Enjoy every second, that is my *law of life*.

Wendy enjoys listening to all kinds of music, as well as playing the piano and attend-ing concerts. She hopes to build a career around children, perhaps designing toys, mak-ing cartoon movies, or opening an amusement park. "We should work hard to reach our goals," Wendy believes, "but we also need to enjoy every second of life."

⌒

THE I*EARN *LAWS OF LIFE* ESSAY PROJECT

Using the Internet, for the past two years students in 26 countries have been writing a *laws of life* essay as a way of sharing their values with each other.

I*EARN (The International Education and Resource Network) uses telecommunica-tions technology to conduct collaborative projects between students and teachers all over the world. When Ed Gragert, Director of I*EARN, heard about the essay program, he realized that students around the world could share their *laws of life* essays with each other online.

This past year, nearly 2,000 essays from over 100 schools in 26 countries and 7 lan-guages were sent via e-mail to I*EARN's *Laws of Life* Newsgroup. Students were invited to read and respond to each others' essays, engaging in a meaningful, cross-cultural dialogue that celebrates the commonality of values around the world.

I*EARN has published *laws of life* teacher materials in Arabic, English, Chinese, French,

Hindi, Russian, and Spanish. Each year, I*EARN features the *laws of life* essays in a multilingual publication that is distributed to classrooms around the world. Students from different countries also have the opportunity to read their essays at I*EARN's International Conference. This past year, the International Conference was held in Beijing, China. ✳

Genevieve Owusu Ansah
age 16

The I*EARN *Laws of Life* Essay Project
GHANA

on HAVING FAITH AND LIVING LIFE SIMPLY
"Life's precious gifts"

THE GREATEST BLESSING is the gift of life. For one to appreciate and enjoy life, it is essential that we recognise the qualities and values that bring out the success and fruitfulness in life. Knowing very well that life is what I make it, and in anything I find myself doing, I will surely reap the harvest one day, good or bad alike. I have searched and worked my way through to keep the best privileges that life can offer.

Personally, from infancy to this present age, one thing that has helped shaped my life is religion. Thus my faith in Christ, which teaches me to obey the word of God. In his words are virtues like honesty, love, truth, generosity, etc., which are all good virtues that if all are to faithfully obey, there will be such peace, unity, and love in the universe. My faith in Christ has helped me look to God alone and at things squarely, hopefully, and with honesty, laughing at impossibilities and crying it out in the midst of all difficulties.

Sincere love shown to me by my family, friends, and neighbours in ways like attention, advice, discipline, counselling, etc., has remarkably helped me stand up to challenges in my life, not wanting to bring shame and dishonour to such precious ones. It makes me know that somebody will always be there to give a hand, comfort, and encourage me even in my weakest, loneliest, and darkest hour. So most times I find myself doing decent things to impress, glorify, honour, and show appreciation for the pure and sincere love and concern shown to me.

Gratitude, which is a secret to a happy living, has greatly impacted my life. It has made me realise that a grateful mind is a great mind, which attracts to itself great things, and that abundance flourishes in a grateful heart. If I want to keep the blessing of life coming to me, I must be grateful for whatever I have and whatever is given, being thankful as well as appreciating great, small, or little things within my possession.

Humility has helped me to accept correction, shortfalls, and weaknesses, and recognise the fact that the largest room I can ever have is a room for improvement. I am not perfect, so I'm able to admit my wrongs and apologise to all, whether matured or young. This makes my friends, neighbours, and family trust me, confide in me as well and share problems together, helping, teaching and learning from each other. Being at their service has made me build up my personality day by day because it pays to be a servant if you want to achieve a lot and become a leader one day.

Despite all the virtues, the one that stands out and always influences the rest is being optimistic. With the feeling of optimism, I look at the events in life with the knowledge that there are both good and bad seasons, but it is better to emphasise and dwell on the best result from the worst conditions. When I'm faced with fear, disappointment, grief, and sorrow, I put positive thinking against negative conditions. I then feel that a strong hand has gripped and taken care of it all; then I feel relieved and serene.

Above all is the virtue of contentment. Life with contentment is a great gain and with that selfishness, jealousy, envy, bitterness, hatred, etc., have no roots. Being content, I get satisfied and happy in life, finding interest in simple things, which have occasionally opened a door to greater opportunities.

The *laws of life* are vast and all will depend on the decisions and choices I make every moment. I make sure that I put on the breast plate of discipline and determination, which has helped me overcome the struggles of life with victory.

This is the first project that Genevieve has participated in on the Internet. She believes that the essay has helped her become aware of her potential as a writer.

❧

I*EARN *LAWS OF LIFE* ESSAY PROJECT
See profile on p. 103

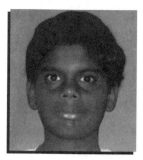

V. Ganesh
age 13

The I*EARN *Laws of Life* Essay Project
INDIA

on THE IMPORTANCE OF LEARNING
"Half knowledge is a dangerous thing"

"LIFE HAS A VALUE only when it has something valuable as its object." From this we can understand that life has many values, but I consider that knowledge is the best value of life.

Desire for power is inherent in man. The love of power comes from the consciousness of man's mental and moral superiority over other created things. It is instinctive, therefore, that man as superior being must control and dominate others. Again the awareness that all men are created unequal gives birth to the desire to rule and dominate others. The history of the world so far as man is concerned is a history of struggle for power. Thus from the primitive wars of tribes and clans to the ruinous wars of today, there is only one idea behind the wars and that is the thirst for power.

Broadly speaking, power is of two kinds—physical and mental. Physical power is of the lower order as compared to the power of the mind. Primitive men mainly understood one kind of power and that was of the body. In the past, the strength of the arms decided things, and might alone was right. However, with the growth of civilization and the development of human mind, the mental power came to be recognized as of the superior order. Mental power has its origin in knowledge.

When man first appeared on the earth he was no better than animals. He was also the beast of prey and was a helpless being, a victim of the wild beast and the hostile forces of nature. But God endowed him with an intelligent mind, and this mind ultimately came to his rescue. He discovered fire and learned its uses, and this knowledge of use of fire gave him power. Similarly, knowledge of other elements and things gradually made him strong. In the course of time his knowledge has achieved wonders in the world and given man mastery over many things.

All the great discoveries and inventions on which modern life is based are but the manifestations of the power of knowledge. The conquest of the forces of nature like water and electricity and the harnessing of these forces for man's use have been made possible by the knowledge of physics. It is the knowledge of mechanics which has lessened distance, broken down the barriers between men, and enabled men to realize the affinity of men all over the world. The epoch-making discoveries of atomic energy have revolutionized the entire concept of future life of man on the earth. Today completely unheard strides made by man in the field of science are the result of the knowledge and perpetual search for wisdom combined with the hunger of power to rule and dominate.

The disadvantages are greater if one reads cheap novels. The life depicted in cheap novels is of a low kind. In fact, the development of art, science, culture and civilization ultimately depends upon knowledge. Nature has yielded her mysteries to this power. It has made physical power and mental strength one and the same. But knowledge has not only given man mental strength, it has taught him how to utilize his physical strength in a better and more and more disciplined and economic way.

Great ideas make great men, and there is no trait more constant in human nature than his habit of pursuing a truth beyond its province. Hence balance is the cardinal virtue. Great as is the power of knowledge, the tendency to misuse it is greater. Knowledge is inclined to fill us with pride. The need is to translate knowledge into wisdom, for knowledge is proud and wisdom is humble. It is only when we have realized this that we understand the significance of knowledge that is power, and get the desire to acquire that knowledge which enables us to find the truth. We must pursue knowledge to its utmost for, "Half knowledge is a dangerous thing; drink deep or taste not the perennial spring."

V. Ganesh enjoys playing the keyboard, reading, listening to music, and collecting stamps, coins, and feathers. He was recently awarded first place in a drawing competition conducted by Tamil Nadu Forest Department.

⌒

I*EARN *LAWS OF LIFE* ESSAY PROJECT
See profile on p. 103

Anne Saab
age 14

The I*EARN *Laws of Life* Essay Project

LEBANON

on BELIEVING IN YOURSELF
"The perfect life"

WHAT IS A PERFECT LIFE? I think of this question a lot. What does it take to be a good person, and to live a life that will never die? I think the answer is living for the person you are, and not for the person others want you to be. When I look around me, I see many people who are afraid of being themselves, especially at my age. Their fear of being unpopular and left out overpowers their dream of becoming the strong and unique people they are. It makes me sad seeing people hide behind masks in fear of being revealed. It seems to me that everybody wants to be something they're not. I want to make a difference and show people that being an individual is the best gift in the world, and we all should be proud of being who we are.

My goal in life is to get the best out of the person I am inside, regardless of the opinions of others. The perfect life for me is a life in which I can live close to myself. I want to explore every aspect within me, not just my physical appearance or intelligence. My strong ambitions for a life like this come from the support I have from my family and friends around me. My parents have always let me be free to make my own decisions and learn from my mistakes. I am forever grateful to them for giving me the opportunity to become the person I am today. My independence has made me a strong person. To live life to the max, one needs to take risks in order to pursue one's dreams. Life is a blessing, and it is up to the individual to make each life worth living, regardless of the situation he or she is in. Although life gets tough at times, it is important to stay in touch with who you are on the inside. I have seen many people at my age who have lost their true selves in the struggle of becoming a part of the world. Seeing this inspires me to work hard at staying myself, and having faith in who I am. The friends I have had through the course of my life have given me courage. They have showed me they care about me, and they appreciate who I am. In turn, I show them that I care about them, and that I wouldn't want them to be anything else but themselves.

The perfect life is up to every individual to achieve. No matter how hard it is to tackle the obstacles of life, one must never lose faith. So whatever people might expect of you, always believe in yourself. One who loses his faith loses everything. Be proud of who you are, forever.

Anne plans to attend college after graduating from high school. On participating in the essay project she shares that "I just wrote down the message I wanted to get through to students my age, which is that your life lies in your own hands, and it becomes whatever you make of it."

⌒

I*EARN *LAWS OF LIFE* **ESSAY PROJECT**
See profile on p. 103

Elisha Reid
age 16

The I*EARN *Laws of Life* Essay Project
AUSTRALIA

on HAPPINESS
"Life has so many wonderful things to offer"

WHEN TOLD ABOUT THIS ESSAY, I had no idea what Ms. Tate meant when she said the *laws of life*. I had never really thought about what I lived by. I started to write an essay about courage, hope, and persistence. I even nearly finished. But they're not my *laws of life*. It took me a whole essay, a few bad days, and a brilliant sunny day for me to realise what my *law of life* really was, and that was happiness.

It's all around us. It's the chirping birds, the playing animals and the clear blue sunny sky. All of which we associate with happiness. It's something I have never thought about. But as I sit here on this beautiful summer day I realise that happiness comes from within. However, those circumstances of others can effect your own happiness if you haven't reached the highest level of true happiness.

Trying to make yourself happy isn't the only way to have a happy life. To make someone else happy from a simple hello, to a hug, to a verbal "I love you," are just simple ways of making others happy and in return make you happy.

Once you have reached that higher level of happiness you have to expect to tumble down at some stages in your life but you can and have to believe that it is possible to regain that sense of happiness. I know many people won't agree with me when I say there is a point of true happiness. Personally I haven't reached that point yet but I believe that someday I will along with all those who do not believe now.

Everyone wants to get the most out of life but occasionally we get blinded by goals which really we only achieve through happiness. I believe in what you put into life is exactly what you will achieve from life; nothing more and nothing less.

I got blinded, blinded by courage, hope, and persistence, and these three things can only be reached through happiness.

Happiness is the base of everything; it's like self-rising flour in a cake; if you haven't got the flour your cake won't rise. When you are happy you don't worry about unimportant things that have bothered you in the past. The bitchiness of the girls next to you just slides right off, the constant nagging from your mum with the state of your room just doesn't bother you. You no longer take in the bad vibes, just the good vibes and all the good things that life has to offer. Life seems so much better and easier to live when you are happy, unlike courage, hope, or persistence. If you're not happy you won't survive. There really is no other way to put it.

Life has so many wonderful things to offer. I believe that when you see the world through eyes of happiness you see the world from a different perspective, a better perspective. Things such as courage, persistence, and hope are only a continuation of happiness and definitely not the *laws of life*, as I first believed. When I am happy and my life is full of happiness I can see the direction my life is taking and the direction that I wish my life to take.

Elisha has won many academic awards. Her future plans are to attend a university and study science. "Participating in the Laws of Life *Essay Project has opened my eyes to a new way of thinking." She adds, "Now I aim to be happy and try not to let things worry me. I now live life to the fullest."*

⌒

I*EARN *LAWS OF LIFE* ESSAY PROJECT
See profile on p. 103

Lisa Jennings
age 19

Fairbanks *Laws of Life* Essay Contest
FAIRBANKS, ALASKA

on LIVING LIFE TO THE FULLEST
"Don't toy with time"

I CRACKED ONE EYE OPEN long enough to glare at the alarm clock and thump it angrily. With the silence restored once again, I huddled back under my mountain of down with a satisfied sigh, convinced in my sleepy state that I had stopped time altogether. No sooner had I drifted back to dreams of Florida beaches than I was rudely jolted back to the reality of the clock buzzing in my ear and the 50° below zero temperatures outside.

I'm sure we would all love to manipulate time—stop it when it's convenient, and speed it up when we get bored. We all know, however, that it's impossible to control the passage of time, and the minutes roll by, often unheeded. For this reason, the most important thing to do is use our time wisely while it's still here. I have found that it's not as easy as say, throwing the alarm clock across the room. To me, making the best use of my time requires a combination of learning from the past, enjoying my time in the present, and planning for my future. It's interesting to see the results of those who either live primarily in the past, those who mold their lives around the present moment, and those who spend vast amounts of time worrying about the future.

A lot of us live our lives wishing we were back in "the good ole days." Elizabeth A. Allen said, "Backward, turn backward, O time in your flight! Make me a child again just for tonight!" It would be nice to stay in a childhood fantasy, but I've had to learn how to accept changes and love life anyway.

I had a wonderful childhood. My family spent our summers running the only sports fishing lodge in the 7.2 million acres of Gates of the Arctic National Park.

Since we could only reach it in my dad's float plane, my childhood from ages two to nine was spent building forts and hiking in beautiful, untouched wilderness. My sister and I taught wild baby birds how to fly, protected our pet dog when he was chased by wolves, and learned the responsibility of caring for guests. We were devastated, however, when in a matter of one year, our lodge was burned down and my dad died in an automobile accident.

My life totally changed now, and it would be very easy to wish myself back to the "good ole days," but I have found that it only inhibits me from getting the benefit of the present. I have learned, through the time I had with my dad, to value the time I have today. It is those who don't see their lives on a larger scale that fall into the second problem of living only for the present moment.

The quest for momentary pleasure has become a widespread pursuit. Las Vegas, Nevada, the gambling center of the world, flaunts not only thousands of arcades, but it ranks first in the nation in suicide, first in divorce, in high school drop-outs, and in homicide against women. It also ranks in the top one-third of the nation in child abuse.

Just recently, about 40 miles from Las Vegas, a seven-year-old girl was raped and strangled in a hotel casino bathroom at 3:48am. Her father, Leroy Iverson, after being warned three times by security guards not to leave her alone in the arcade, left her there while he gambled. Even after she was killed, it was said that her father tried to cut a deal with the hotel. "He said he wouldn't sue anybody if they would give him $100 to gamble with, free beer and fly his girlfriend in from out of town."

This man gambled not only his belongings, but his child's life as well. Have we, as a nation, become so calloused that we can no longer see that the pursuit of momentary happiness is not only often based on chance, but is also destructive to ourselves and those surrounding us? We pay for it when we don't view our lives outside of the present moment.

Being a young person, it would be easy to live my life the way I feel like right now and forget about the consequences, but I am the only one who's determining my future. I want to make something of myself by taking the future into consideration and using my time accordingly.

Some people take it a little too far, however, and spend so much time worrying about the future that they can't even enjoy life. I know of a group that lived near Chitina, Alaska years ago. They were named the Iveys. They spent most of their time storing food in preparation of hard times. Since that was their main focus, they had a cave in the side of a mountain which they filled with food. Not long ago, the mountain shifted and their cave collapsed, swallowing up their life's work. Devastated, the group fell apart.

I'm convinced that these people sold themselves short of happiness by centering their whole lives around what could possibly happen. It's too easy to forget to value the things that really matter, such as friends and family.

Once I heard someone say, "The journey is the destination." Since this is the only moment we have control over, it ought to be cherished, with the recognition that it is building our future bit by bit; otherwise our lives will be empty carcasses of what could have been. Will we be blown aimlessly along in this journey, or will we take advantage of our time enough to use it wisely? We make the choice every day to either linger in the past or learn from it. We choose between the thrill of momentary pleasure or the life-long happiness found in considering the consequences. We can choose to view a seemingly intangible future through eyes of anxiety, or we can recognize that the future is, indeed, a result of each moment lived right now. Tomorrow the alarm will ring like it always does and we will be faced with the choice to either close our eyes and shut off the time signals or wake up and take advantage of the minutes of the day.

Lisa plans to have a career in the medical field. "Writing this essay and taking part in this contest," she shares, "was an opportunity to settle for myself what I deem to be important and to be sure enough about my ideas to communicate them clearly to others."

⟜

FAIRBANKS *LAWS OF LIFE* ESSAY CONTEST

"This is great! Kids get a chance to say what's in their hearts!" That is how contest coordinator Corky Dow felt when he heard about the essay contest in 1998. After learning about the program at the Kiwanis International Convention, Mr. Dow brought the contest to his community of Fairbanks.

The community has responded enthusiastically, and many local businesses and community leaders have gotten involved in the contest. Contest sponsors include Chena Kiwanis Club, Dow Financial Services, Edward Jones Brokerage, Fairbanks Lions Club, Kiwanis Club of Fairbanks, Mt. McKinley Bank, Soroptomists of Fairbanks, Mr. and Mrs. Clutts, and many other private donors.

Each year, volunteers from the chamber of commerce select the prizewinning essays. The awards ceremony is held at a Kiwanis meeting, during which the top finalists receive cash prizes and read their essays. In Fairbanks, the contest is a community event that can claim to be the "Farthest North Essay Contest!" ✳

Vassily Polyvianny
age 12

Russia *Laws of Life* Essay Contest

RUSSIAN FEDERATION

on LIVING BY YOUR VALUES
"The laws of life will continue to influence my life"

WHAT IS A LAW? A dictionary defines it as a common set of rules established by a state. Each individual in society should accept legal laws and follow them. What then is a *law of life*? In my view it is a set of personal rules that one should reflect upon and set out to live by.

When exploring the evolution of legal laws we may assume that they derive from previous common experiences and situations. Similar to that, setting up personal *laws of life* is related to thinking about past situations and mistakes and searching for better solutions.

What are the *laws of life* to me? I started investigating the topic only now, when I am 12 year old. I believe that to determine my *laws of life* that will give me guidance I have to learn how to live in harmony with those around me, with my family and with myself. I also have to learn how to use the past mistakes and obstacles as useful tools that help me live through.

It seems that it works as a sort of pattern where law = my relations with others (teachers, friends) + my relations with my family (mother, father, grandmother and grandfather) + my relations with myself (I and I).

To get along with my family I should keep in mind the situations that could be stressful and cause trouble to those who I love. If I do my best to please my family everybody will benefit. Therefore the Law #1 is: *Try to please others, and joy will return to you two or three times as much.*

Now, my relations with myself... When I get a low grade I am frustrated, but as soon as I start thinking of the situation as a challenge that I face (as for example, Peter the Great who took obstacles as benefits to grow), I feel better. My Law #2 is: *Don't be afraid of problems. Problems can always be overcome and make you stronger, and you benefit by paving the way to higher goals.*

My relations with those around me... I noticed a long time ago, that if I worry about somebody's negative judgments I am pleasing those who want to hurt me. My Law #3 is: *Be in harmony with yourself, don't worry about negative attitudes, and those who try to hurt you will get hurt back.*

Well, this Law does not seem to fit well with my Law #4: *Don't wish bad things on those around you...* I should think thoroughly on that.

I am 12 years old, and, if God allows, I will be 13 and so on . . . I am convinced my *laws of life* will develop with time and continue to influence my life.

P.S. Finishing the essay, I turned over a vase with flowers on my dad's desk and some of his papers got wet. Dad is not home now and I am not sure what he would say or do when coming back. Which of his laws would he apply? Which of my laws will I use? Seems that I need to add a new law to my set of rules. Law #5 says: *Don't let the harm you caused to others grow and expand. Do your very best to improve the situation as soon as possible.* [Translated from Russian]

Vassily would like to become a doctor, specifically a nose and throat specialist. He enjoys playing guitar, hiking, and sightseeing. Vassily shares that "Writing a laws of life essay was an opportunity for me to think seriously about the things that really matter for determining my lifestyle, my relations with my family and those around me, and with myself."

RUSSIA *LAWS OF LIFE* ESSAY CONTEST

Junior Achievement (JA) Russia is a nonprofit organization that since 1991 has been teaching young Russians about the moral and spiritual foundations that underpin the free enterprise system. Over one million Russian students participated in JA programs during the 1999-2000 academic year.

Under the dynamic leadership of JA Russia executive director Nina Kuznetsova, the essay contest is held in schools and lyceums in 30 regions of the Russian Federation. This past year more than 10,000 Russian students wrote a *laws of life* essay!

Two hundred distinguished Russian officials, diplomats, business leaders, educators, and family members of the prizewinning students attended the spring 2000 awards ceremony, which was held in Moscow at the prestigious Central House of Journalists. Cash prizes totaling $8,200 were awarded to the 18 top finalists and their teachers.

During the ceremony, The Honorable James Collins, American Ambassador to Russia, remarked: "After reading the *laws of life* essays, I now know that the future of Russia is in good hands." ✷

Amy Schnelle
age 17

Medford Kiwanis
Laws of Life Essay Contest

MEDFORD, WISCONSIN

on COURAGE
"Overcoming fear"

As I look back on my many years of triumph and defeat, one particular incident stands out. It wasn't the outcome of this situation, but the lesson I learned that is important. It was the lesson of confronting my fears and it will stick with me for the rest of my life.

It was a cold winter day in January. I was in sixth grade and in addition to my studies I participated in the band program. The beginning of the year had gone smoothly, but as most students progressed, I seemed to be regressing. My teacher had an opinion that it was a good idea to have students play their lessons in front of all the other students. I did not agree with this theory, because of the fear it instilled.

The day of lessons came and I was overwhelmed with fear. I forgot to practice my lesson and knew I would mess up and look like a fool. I rode the bus over to the middle school, clenching my clarinet in anguish. I walked in the door feeling my heart jump out of my throat. I knew it was too late and I was stuck. I sat down and took out my clarinet. I was shaking so badly, that I could hardly put the reed in place. Everyone else played his or her lesson and finally it was my turn.

I placed the clarinet in my mouth and blew out my lesson. My tone was good, but my rhythms were another story. "Did you practice your lesson?" the teacher barked at me.

"Well I...I," I muttered

"I thought so," she replied, as she gave me an evil glaring look. I felt so humiliated and ashamed. My world had come crashing down in an instant. My love for playing the clarinet was shattered and my dreams of playing forever lost.

From that point on, I hated playing the clarinet. I kept getting worse and worse. The day before my next lesson I took out my clarinet and tried to play, but I couldn't get any sound out. I tried and struggled, but to no avail. I was so upset I started to cry. I thought to myself, "why am I putting myself through this torture?" And I resolved to quit.

The day of the new lessons came up and I knew I wouldn't be able to play, because I was so terrible. In a moment of panic, I told the teacher I was sick and went to the office to call home. When all the other students left to go to band, I stayed waiting for my mom to pick me up. It was so relieving and such an easy way out. I didn't know why, but for some reason, hiding from my fear seemed to relieve my guilt, self-hatred and remarkably my fears altogether. I resolved at that moment that all of life's problems could be dealt with by suppressing them until they go away.

The avoidance of my lessons continued for some time until my mom demanded that I practice before I could go outside. I finally confessed that I couldn't play and that I wasn't sick and I wanted to quit. I hadn't even opened my mouth before the tears started flowing. "I hate clarinet and I hate band. I just want to quit," I squeaked.

"Well," my mom said. "If you really hate it and really want to quit, then why are you crying?" She had a point and I realized that I wanted to stay in band and, by not facing my fears, I had created a black hole that would be more difficult to climb out of now. I fabricated a resolution not to hide from my fears and to stand up to even the worst of them, so a solution could be achieved. I agreed to meet with my other band teacher after school the next day.

I went in and told her that I was having a problem and couldn't figure out why. She sat down with me and went over all the keys to find a leak or torn pad. I was very surprised that she didn't just yell at me for not practicing. Then she had me play for her. The tears started to roll again and I tried, but only a squeak came out. She looked at me in my present situation and told me to wait in the room. She left the room and returned in a flash. She asked me to play again and as I tried she grabbed the clarinet by the bell and pulled it downward.

"Aha," she said and she told me that I was squeezing the reed. She handed me a new reed. A 3½, I thought to myself. How could I play a 3½ if I couldn't even play a 2½ like everyone else? Nonetheless, I tried and to my surprise, I could play. Just like before and even better. My problem was solved and my fear removed.

That year I improved a lot and by the end of the year, I switched to the bass clarinet. I've been playing the bass ever since and I love playing it. Now when I look back on that time, I'm so glad that I faced my fear and stayed in band. I could have missed some of the best times of my life.

Overcoming fear is an important *law of life* for a very important reason. Fear can consume everything in a person's life and overcoming it takes courage and commitment. Hiding from those very fears only digs a hole, which makes a person stay trapped inside their fear. After facing a fear, life can become easier to deal with and much more enjoyable. After all sometimes the things that are feared the most are the things that are most important.

Amy plans to attend college and pursue her interest in either computer science or biology. She recently received a Young Poets Writing Award and a Gold Medal in the Science Olympiad.

MEDFORD KIWANIS *LAWS OF LIFE* ESSAY CONTEST

The Medford Kiwanis heard about the essay contest at the National Kiwanis Convention in 1999 and knew it would be a great fit for their community. Soon, the district superintendent was on board, and ever since, the contest has been a key part of the district's character education programs.

Under the leadership of character education coordinator Jackie Strick, the essay contest was launched in the spring of 1999 at the Medford Area Middle School for 7th and 8th graders and has since expanded to include the high school's juniors as well. Each year, $2,400 in savings bonds is awarded to the top prizewinners.

From the contest's inception, the Medford Kiwanis have raised funds for the contest from a variety of sponsors, including Hurd Millwork, Medford Kiwanis, Mid-Wisconsin Bank, Taylor Credit Union, and Time Federal Savings Bank. ✳

Jesse Gordon
age 18

Livingston Parish
Laws of Life Essay Contest

LIVINGSTON PARISH, LOUISIANA

on PERSEVERANCE
"The greatest law of life"

O NE OF THE GREATEST LAWS OF LIFE that I have learned is, "I can not give up on life even if the situation is horribly hopeless." I must go on and live, and try to overcome it. My life has value. I should try to be happy, and I must learn how to deal with whatever life throws at me. I must not give up on anyone, because no matter how hard it gets, someone out there still cares and loves me.

I have been in a situation that most people do not think about. Many people just turn their heads and do not want to believe it exists. Some people, when I try to talk to them, just tell me it is not as bad as it seems, and do not listen. But the truth of the matter is I need to tell someone, because if I hold it in it will just build up and make matters worse.

Life is not hopeless like I thought it was. I was not even sure if I should be here in this world. I even doubted God because of the way I was treated. I started blaming my mother for allowing me to be beaten and severely punished for little things that I should have done, like feed the dog. One day, it was about 3:00 and I forgot to feed the dog. My punishment was that I could not eat for 24 hours. I blamed my mother because she stayed in that situation and let herself and her kids be treated horribly.

Another example of this treatment was when I was eight years old. It was seven days before Christmas. At 6:00 a.m. my biological father woke up me and my sister, who was seven, to clean the yard, which was full of his beer cans and trash. My sister and I thought the yard was pretty clean, so we went inside and turned on the television. We were watching the television when my biological father came in and started hollering and screaming and cursing my sister and me. He said we did not listen and were lazy. He said because there was one little piece of paper under the steps, there would not be Christmas. That year we did not have Christmas.

Another example is when I was nine years old, my biological father asked me for a tool while he was working on the van. I did not know what tool it was that he asked for, so I stood there. He got up and hollered, "Why didn't you give me the tool?" I simply said I did not know what tool it was. He hit me and started screaming. He said that I have seen him working on the van before, and someone else had handed it to him, so I should have known what tool he wanted. I got grounded to my room for one week.

My life has been like that, and more than most can imagine, from the day I could crawl to the day my mom left. I was thirteen years old before I could have friends over to my home. I was thirteen before I did not have to be scared when I woke up. I was thirteen before I could ask questions without fear. I was thirteen before I could eat ice cream with my mother and stepdad. My biological father would eat ice cream in front of me and my sister and not let us eat any. I soon realized that my mother was scared for herself and for her kids; she did not know what to do. God finally gave her the strength and courage to get out of a bad situation.

In the past, I have had a bad attitude toward life because of the way I was raised. I treated people bad, those I loved and those I did not know. I blamed it on the way I was raised. I had a short temper and did not respect authority. However, I have learned that I could sit here all day making up excuses. But the truth be known, I have realized that I have the power to change. I have the power to be a different person in life. I do not have to be like my biological father. I can treat others well, and not have a short temper and bad attitude with everyone. I have discovered that others will treat me well if I treat them well, which means having more friends.

I started treating others better. My mother is now married to a great man. Life is wonderful. I do not think life is hopeless and not worth living anymore. I have realized that I am happy, and I am glad that I did not give up on life. Last year, for the first time, I had a 4.0 on my final report card. I now have many friends, because I stuck with it. I pulled through a horribly hopeless situation, and things are not hopeless anymore.

Jesse recently won a National Science Merit Award and is featured in Who's Who Among American High School Students.

LIVINGSTON PARISH *LAWS OF LIFE* ESSAY CONTEST

Sometimes it helps to read the fine print. That's what Anita Davis, drug education coordinator for the parish, realized when she contacted the Center for Youth Issues (CYI) after reading about the contest in a CYI newsletter. The goals of the program appealed to Ms. Davis, and she immediately began promoting the contest to area high schools.

The Livingston Parish Contest was launched during the 1999-2000 school year and was sponsored by the CYI, local school board, and private community donations. In the very first year of the contest, more than 5,100 students wrote a *laws of life* essay! Eight area schools took part in the contest: Albany, Denham Springs Freshman, Denham Springs High, Doyle, Holden, Live Oak, Springfield, and Walker.

The awards banquet was held at Crawford's Restaurant where students read their winning essays and received awards from the Livingston Parish superintendent of education and the Livingston Parish school board president.

With such an extraordinary first year, the citizens of Livingston Parish have a lot to be proud of! ✳

Lindi Davis
age 16

Napa County Commission on Self-Esteem
Laws of Life Essay Contest

NAPA COUNTY, CALIFORNIA

on KINDNESS
"Say a kind word to someone else at least once a day"

FEW KIDS TODAY are taught the value of empathy. It seems so hard for people to have compassion toward others and to actually understand what they are going through.

I was raised in a very loving family. As a child I was taught to put others before myself. We were always told to go out of our way to make someone else happy. My mom would tell me to say at least one kind word to someone every day. I will admit that it wasn't always very easy to do. But as soon as you see the look of gratitude in that person's eyes you just want to do as much as you possibly can.

I had an experience with a guy that I knew where people were always making fun of him. He was the guy that everyone liked to pick on. Because he was home taught, the only people he knew were the ones that he went to church with. Even there I would see people being mean to him. Every time I saw that happening I knew in my heart that it was wrong. From that moment on I decided I would make an effort to be his friend. I started taking him places with me and introducing him to people. I could tell by just doing that I was making him so happy. And I loved the fact that I was really making a difference in his life. For a while people were giving me a bad time for hanging around him. But it didn't matter to me, because I knew that what I was doing was right.

After a while I realized that he wasn't the kind of person everybody thought he was. And I was lucky to have him as a friend. And to this day we are still really good friends. People have almost completely stopped making fun of him. But the weird thing is that he never changed. What had changed was the hearts of others around him.

From this experience I've learned to be more loving and to show a little more empathy toward other people. What I did for my friend was so easy to do. And at the same time I had a lot of fun. I could only hope that others would start following my example. Before you start judging someone try to find out who he or she really is. You might be surprised. I want to make it a goal for everyone to say a kind word to someone else at least once a day. I can promise you that it will be the best feeling you ever get, knowing that one word could make someone's day a little brighter.

Lindi plans to attend college and study physical therapy. She explains, "Writing a laws of life *essay has showed me that people still notice when someone is being kind toward others. I hope that when people read my essay they will want to follow my example."*

⌒

NAPA COUNTY COMMISSION ON SELF-ESTEEM
LAWS OF LIFE ESSAY CONTEST

In Napa County, California, the essay contest is a perfect fit for the Commission on Self-Esteem, an organization dedicated to the personal growth and well being of all people. The Napa County Board of Supervisors also recognizes the contest as an important character education program that benefits students. Together, the Commission on Self-Esteem and the County Board of Supervisors co-sponsor the essay contest.

First launched in the fall of 1999, the contest was promoted to English teachers throughout Napa County, and students from six area high schools participated in the contest: Napa, Calistoga, Vintage, New Technology, Chamberlain, and Temescal. Superintendent of Schools Barbara Nemko emceed the awards ceremony, which was held at the Napa Elks Lodge. The 11 finalists were given cash prizes totaling more than $4,000 in the form of U.S. Savings Bonds. Prizes began at $100 and the grand prizewinner was awarded $2,000!

Reverend Hal Milton, chair of the Commission on Self-Esteem, explains why the contest is such a winning program in Napa County: "Ultimately, the contest is about concerned adults in our community working together to support, honor, and publicly recognize young people who reflect upon and write about their personal beliefs and values. The contest benefits us all—students, families, schools, and the community as a whole." ✳

Katharine Boicourt
age 15

Talbot County *Laws of Life* Essay Contest
TALBOT COUNTY, MARYLAND

on OPTIMISM
AND LIVING LIFE TO THE FULLEST
"If nothing else, these will build character"

THERE ARE MANY MORALS or *laws of life* that people live by, but I have chosen two that I believe to be the most important. The first is to be encouraging, no matter the circumstances. One must go out of one's way to be kind to people whether it be an enemy or a best friend. The people I like the most all have this trait in common. They listen without judging you and truly care about what you are saying. Another law is to not put life into a too-perfect monotonous script. Spontaneity and the ability to try new things can apply to many aspects of life.

One great example regarding the first law is the father of a friend of mine. He had a chronic heart problem caused by his involvement in the Vietnam War. The first time I met him, I realized what a good-natured and genuine person he was. He always kept a smile on his face. Within a year of moving here, he knew every person in his son's class and had something good to say to everyone. When his condition worsened, he kept on giving to people. His gifts were not in the literal sense but in that he complimented people, and continued to raise others' spirits. Not thinking about his physical limitations, he tried to make the best of his situation. Beneath the exterior of a frail man with a heart pump was a man who was young at heart and supported everyone. I remember that at his son's birthday party he came outside despite the cold. He made an effort to greet everybody and asked to be updated on our lives without mention of his own. Though he knew his chances to live a long life were slim, he put aside his personal concerns and gave himself in full to others. His decision to enjoy life actively and encourage others rather than watch it pass by shows courage and strength. This also shows how such a law can be so essential. Luckily, he has had a successful transplant since then. It is this selfless honesty and compassion for people that I truly respect. I know that anyone who knows him feels the same way. By being optimistic, he not only made himself feel better, but others as well. By example, he has reinforced my belief in this *law of life*.

Concerning my second law, being unpredictable and experiencing new things is also important. As the father in the cartoon Calvin & Hobbes always said, "If nothing else, it will build character." By being spontaneous, you may not always win, and sometimes you will lose big, but it is this very experience that builds character. Some of the most unique and interesting people are always looking to experience all aspects of life. My friend Barbara was such a person. She was one of those people that in numbers had many years but in mind and outlook was ageless. At first impression, her attitude could be intimidating. However, she was one of the most interesting and understanding people that I have ever known. Every time my family visited her, she had a new story to tell or a new gadget to show us. These things that she tried reflected everything about her in that she experimented with all and chose to absorb it with great interest. Not just materially did she do this, but with people as well. She knew and took interest in all kinds of people, and they responded and were influenced. Barbara had a passion for irregularity in life; she had tried it all from feng shui to hunting doves. It seemed that her life had bits and pieces of every attribute she ever liked in people. In this way her practice of spontaneity had influenced the formation of her character. I think that in experiencing new things, we can become more compassionate for that which we do not know. As a result, life becomes more entertaining and joyful.

The reason I believe so strongly in these laws is that I find those who I most admire have these characteristics. In abiding by them, I hope to improve my character and to make an impact on those I meet. Without others' optimism and faith in humankind we would be lost in hopelessness, and without spontaneity there would be no fun and intrigue in life.

Kate plays soccer, basketball, and runs track for her school. She also likes to ride horses on the weekends.

⌒

TALBOT COUNTY *LAWS OF LIFE* ESSAY CONTEST

Sponsor Tom Hill is very clear about why he got involved in the contest. "Sir John Templeton is a personal hero of mine. I've been inspired by his commitment to passing on life's most valuable lessons."

The essay contest is in its second year in Talbot County. Financial support comes from Mr. Hill as well as from the Youth and Community Fund of Easton Rotary. Character Counts! Mid-Shore Community, an organization dedicated to character education and development, also sponsors the contest as a program that brings the community together to celebrate young people.

The contest is open to middle and high school students in the county's schools. Judging the essays are individuals from the Easton Rotary, Rotaract, The Harbor Club, and Soroptomist International of Talbot County. ✹

Lindsay Braman
age 18

College of the Ozarks
Laws of Life Essay Contest
POINT LOOKOUT, MISSOURI

on HELPING OTHERS, PASSION, AND INTEGRITY
"Eight birds, two mountains, and one big yellow Chevy Malibu"

I am convinced my life belongs to the whole community; and as long as I live, it is my privilege to do for it whatever I can, for the harder I work, the more I live. I rejoice in life for its own sake. Life is no brief candle to me. It is a sort of splendid torch which I got hold of for a moment, and I want to make it burn brightly as possible before turning it over to future generations.

THESE ARE THE WORDS of George Bernard Shaw. In a few short sentences Shaw sums up everything that I, for years, have tried to define so inarticulately. I began high school as a shy, pudgy girl, the girl hiding behind stringy brown locks of hair and who wore the same nondescript gray tennis shoes every day. At this point in my life, this quote would have meant little if anything to me. I had no concept of service or passion and had no great theory on honor. At this point, selfish and materialistic didn't even begin to describe me. Watching from the sidewalk as my newly licensed peers zoomed by in their new cars, I felt nothing but pity for myself and contempt for the world around me for not giving me what I thought I was entitled to. Despite my selfishness through my early teenage years, somehow I never lost a sense of compassion I was blessed to have picked from my now weathered, silver-haired father. Through luck or the grace of God, amazing people were somehow drawn to me. I was blessed to meet several people who showed me what it was to be, quite simply, a human being. Shaw states that the goal in life is to be capable of hard work, to live boldly, and to gain a passion for life, that will live on long after your last breath on this earth. With these words he conveys the three characteristics of what I believe to be the timeless, unadulterated qualities that define each and every one of us: willingness to serve, passion, and, probably most important, integrity.

When I was younger, maybe five or six, every Wednesday afternoon I waited inside the front window of my family's house with my eyes glued to the speck where the road appeared from over the hill nearby. When my grandma's banana yellow Malibu finally topped the hill I would jump to my feet and run out the door before the car could even come to a stop in our driveway. Grandma Cressie and I had a date every Wednesday at 4:00; we never missed the weekly story hour at the dilapidated and smelly old public library. I still remember how the storyteller could take me absolutely anywhere just with her words and my imagination, I remember how this hour was the best hour of my entire week, but I remember amazingly few specific stories. The one story I do remember well enough to retell now is a Native American story describing their beliefs about how the birds came to be respected in the hierarchy that they are. Everyone knows that the eagle is the most majestic bird, but few people know of the tale describing how he claimed this position. Many years ago, before there were humans upon this earth, the animals roamed free. The birds, being the only animals able to fly, roamed freely over the skies. One day, the birds decided they needed a leader; after much argument, they decided they would choose a leader according to who could fly the highest. All at once the birds leapt into the sky. Slowing first was the chickadee; his wings were far too small to carry him very high. Next the robin fell back, leaving only the blue jay, eagle, hawk, owl, and vulture still rising. Slowly they all dropped down until only the eagle and the owl were left. Both were growing extremely tired as they soared higher to the cheers of the other birds. One moment before they were both about to give up, the birds left on the ground saw a tiny speck rise from the back of the eagle just as he began to lose altitude. The birds cheered madly as they realized the speck was the sparrow, rising high above, thanks to the lift from the eagle. Immediately, the birds chose the eagle as their leader because he had borne the weight of another bird when he, alone, could have easily overtaken the owl. Despite the physical burden of helping another achieve his best, he chose selflessly to help the sparrow and sacrifice his chance of winning the competition. To this day, the eagle remains a sign of inspiration and motivation. George Bernard Shaw says it is a privilege to help others when you belong to a community. I believe one of the greatest *laws of life* is to understand our responsibility to a community much greater than ourselves and to learn to sacrifice ourselves for others. It's fairly easy to serve others with our hands but there are totally different aspects of service that many people overlook. Service is not just helping an elderly woman with her groceries or volunteering in a children's ward at a hospital; service is something you do with every part of your being. We must also have the ability to listen. I feel that listening is the single best service we can provide to anyone. We must develop an ear that can listen not only to words but can truly hear the strength, compassion, and humility to take action.

In eighteen years of wandering, I've met people who were honest, altruistic, and hard working, but for some reason had not impacted the world the way they could have. It was in thinking of that that I added passion to my list of *laws of life*. People with character have a respect for rules, but they are also fascinated with creative answers to life's little problems. People with character do not scale for "right" answers; they create pathways to their own solutions. People with character question, challenge, and change the world. People with strong morals but who still remember humanity are willing to do whatever it takes to leave the world even slightly better than when they found it. Shaw compares life to a flame, not just any flame, but a bright, blazing torch. This comparison is one that I love. Several months ago I had a life changing experience at National Leadership Camp in backcountry Colorado. As I sat in an open air chapel erected near the top of a mountain and breathed in the August air chilled by the night and the high altitude, I heard some of the most ordinary-seeming people say the most amazing things I have ever heard in my life. As Sharon, our director, slowly mounted the steps to the podium I could not take my eyes off the amazing view of the Mummy Range and the moon slowly rising above it. When Sharon arrived at the podium she turned to look at the view as well before pointing up to the first star that had appeared in the sky and said, "Each of you have a flame inside you. It is much like this star." There was a pregnant pause for emphasis before Sharon continued: "As the night grows darker, this star will grow brighter... until morning, when the sky will lighten and we will no longer need the stars to navigate by. The flame inside of you is very similar; you shall serve as a beacon of light to those around you. When the world appears to have grown dark, you will show others the fire. Your fire will grow brighter and brighter until the day you are no longer needed or are needed more someplace else." I think that Shaw believes, as I do, that a flame represents passion, and the larger the flame, the more powerful and insatiable the passion. Shaw knows that the darkness of the entire world cannot extinguish the light of a single candle, nor can a world of skepticism darken the heart of a believer. Like every National Leadership Camp delegate before me, I light a candle each night to remind myself of the passion that I have and to reconnect me to the lights that I know exist across the country.

A few years ago, I was able to take a state and local government class from a veteran Kansas State Legislator named Rex. Rex spent twenty-five years in the Kansas State Legislature and was there when the death penalty was under heavy debate. One night at class Rex asked his class of three students at the local community college what the "honest" thing was to do: vote what his conscience was screaming at him, or vote what his constituents favored. Morally and religiously, Rex knew what to do, but he also knew his job was to accurately reflect the views of those he represented. It was then that I realized just how difficult the position of being an honest leader was. We often think that an honest day's work is an easy thing to do, but the fact is that for many people it is not. Finally, each of us must have a self-defined sense of what integrity is. Whatever religion we follow, whatever belief system we were raised with, at the end of the day we must be at peace with our actions and ourselves, and I believe that in most cases, integrity develops only through hard work and trial and error. Through my experience in student leadership and coordinating student projects, the projects I learned the most from were the projects I poured my blood, sweat, and tears into and then failed. I learned to admit my mistakes, pick myself back up, and move on. I once met a man, Jamie Clark, who had a passion for climbing and had recently climbed Mount Everest—only the eighth Canadian to ever do so. The interesting thing about Jamie was that he had failed twice before finally reaching the summit on the third attempt. Each attempt his team made took two to three years of training and fundraising before they could try again. Jamie developed his character and integrity because he refused to give up despite normally crippling injuries and amazing odds against him. Each time his team tried the ascent they learned more, and though failing twice was heartbreaking they improved more each time, and their third attempt was one of the fastest climbs of Mount Everest ever.

These qualities, willingness to serve, passion, and integrity, are what define us. Unfortunately, these qualities in a person are very hard to develop without actual real life experience; they are characteristics that develop, most of the time, in our darkest hours. I've come a long way from the hidden, quiet girl who yearned for a pair of name brand shoes and a new car. Today, I am the outgoing woman who believes every word worth speaking should be said with enthusiasm and who plans on joining the Peace Corps before getting any traditional job after college. Looking back, I realize even the examples I have presented were not the life changing moments that developed my character; rather, they were moments I looked upon for guidance and inspiration when I hit rock bottom. Character is something we find inside ourselves in our most desperate times and something that defines every action we make.

Lindsay plans to obtain her B.A. and then serve in the Peace Corps. She shares, "It is incredibly encouraging to know that there are people out there who recognize that many members of my generation are actually of strong moral character and integrity."

⟡

COLLEGE OF THE OZARKS *LAWS OF LIFE* ESSAY CONTEST

A student's introduction to character development begins the first day he or she arrives at College of the Ozarks. This 1,500 student liberal arts college kicks off each fall semester with a two-week Character Camp for incoming freshmen. The purpose of the camp is to provide not only an orientation to the College's facilities, but also an opportunity for students to learn about the values upon which College of the Ozarks was established. The essay contest is a highlight of the two-week experience. The contest is sponsored by the College, with additional support from Willard and Pat Walker.

Writing a *laws of life* essay gives incoming freshmen a chance to express their own core values. College of the Ozarks English faculty judge the essays, and winners are announced at an awards banquet held during Character Camp. The *laws of life* essay becomes part of each student's academic portfolio. On the eve of their graduation, these students will be provided with a copy of their essay and asked to respond to the question, "Are these values still most important to you?"

According to President Jerry Davis, "At College of the Ozarks, we put character on the front burner from the time students first arrive and keep drawing attention to it throughout their college careers. The *Laws of Life* Essay Contest is a key part of our character development programs." ✳

Neil Diaz
age 19

Joseph Family Foundation
Laws of Life Essay Contests

SOUTHERN CALIFORNIA

on LOVE
"Nurturing love in a flower pot"

ONE'S MORALS AND IDEALS are like a seed being planted. I make that comparison because I think that everything in life is part of a process like the growth of a seed is a process. Seeds are planted in a flower pot full of soil. Then ingredients are placed inside the flower pot, each with its own importance in determining the seeds' growth. What also helps determine the seeds' growth is the love and care shown. Without love and care there's not much to look forward to.

As I mentioned before, a seed in a flower pot full of soil is what I compared my morals and ideals to. The flower pot in itself is the foundation, and it's also a big part of the development of the seed's growth. I see my mother as my foundation. She has raised me to become a respectful, caring young man. She has also instilled values in me; she has shown me the importance of them and why I should follow those values. One of the most important things my mother has taught me is to love myself as well as others.

Next would be the soil placed inside the flower pot. The soil signifies the surroundings of the seed. The soil also nurtures the seed, allowing it to know it's loved. The soil in my life is my family and friends. Their love for me has shown me great examples of how to be kind and loving toward others. My family has also placed me in a great environment, surrounded by people who care and are very loving.

Now after the soil has been set you would have to place the seed. The seed in this essay would be me. I am growing and will continue to grow as long as I live by the morals I was taught. My mother as well as my family and friends have helped me prosper just as my values and beliefs will help me be successful and happy in life. One other very important ingredient that the seed needs is water. Water allows the seed to develop into a strong, well-oriented flower. Love is my water and it's something I receive every day from my family. I think love is essential to a person; without love we cannot mature or be happy.

Last, but not least, is the sun. The sun is the last ingredient a seed needs to grow. The sun is what brings happiness to the flower and gives it energy. This is how I feel when I am with the people I love and care for. Despite all of the sun's energy, there comes a period in time where the clouds overcome the sun and do not allow it to shine. The clouds resemble the problems I've faced in life. Not having my father in my life has been the biggest cloud of them all. His absence in my life has made me really hateful toward him at times. But if I have learned anything from that it is that you need to learn how to forgive. Without forgiveness a person cannot go on in life without some kind of pain in his or her heart. I have also learned that every day is a new day, and we should live for the future and not for what happened in the past.

Neil plans to attend college and receive a degree in fire science. In 2000, he was a proud recipient of the Best Sportsmanship Award. "The Laws of Life *Essay Contest has not only made me realize what I truly believe in," he explains, "but most importantly, it has made me realize the morals my mother has instilled in me."*

⌒

JOSEPH FAMILY FOUNDATION *LAWS OF LIFE* ESSAY CONTESTS

In 1998, while attending a Young Presidents' Organization meeting in Atlanta, Georgia, Mike Joseph and Steve Colwell (the Joseph Family Foundation's first executive director) shared their commitment to young people with Sir John Templeton, who suggested they take an information packet on the essay contest and read it on the plane ride back to California. As they read through the packet, they realized that the essay contest was a perfect fit for their family foundation, whose mission is dedicated to helping children live healthy, fulfilling, spiritual lives and strengthening the bonds of family. And so the Joseph Family Foundation Contests were born!

In the spring of 1999, the Joseph Family Foundation began sponsoring the essay contest at three southern California high schools. With the help of Lynn Joseph (the Foundation's new executive director), the contests have expanded to seven high schools from Los Angeles to San Diego. Steve Colwell, who is still on the Joseph Family Foundation Board and is now the Executive Director of the Wilcox Foundation, has also come on board to sponsor a special contest at Carlsbad High School for 9th and 10th graders. This past year, the two Foundations awarded over $30,000 in prize money to 56 students and teachers. Participating schools include Carlsbad High School, El Camino High School, John Marshall Secondary Fundamental School, John Muir High School, Oceanside High School, Salesian High School, and William Blair High School.

Sponsor Lynn Joseph believes that the contest fills a critical gap in a young person's education: "In four years of high school, students are asked to write many mandatory assignments. Rarely are they asked to write about their deepest thoughts and strongest beliefs. Young people all have wonderful stories about family, friendship, God, love, compassion, and challenges; they want to tell us these stories, and we want to hear them." ✳

Jessica Atwell
age 17

Joseph Family Foundation
Laws of Life Essay Contests
SOUTHERN CALIFORNIA

on HELPING OTHERS
"Everyone can make a difference"

"HOLA NINO, como te llamas?" I asked.

"Jorge," he answered sheepishly.

"Feliz Navidad, Jorge!" I added. I could tell by the way that he held on to me that he hadn't been picked up in a long time. "Cuantos anos tienes, mijo?" I asked him.

"Tres," he uttered with a smile and a show of fingers.

As he held on to my shoulder and gripped me tightly, I scanned the view in front of me. I stood in the middle of a few run-down buildings assembled as a makeshift Mexican orphanage. It sat perched on the side of a dirt hill overlooking the cardboard shacks and houses so many people call home.

The second that I had stepped out of the air-conditioned Jeep Cherokee and into the dusty Tijuana air, the children had come running. They smiled and chattered in Spanish so quickly that I could hardly understand what they were saying. The first to approach me and reach to be picked up was little Jorge. He scarcely let go of me until I had to leave and even then he cried. The afternoon I would spend with him would have a great impact on my life as well as help me to realize one of the most important lessons I have ever learned.

Four years ago, I joined Carlsbad High School's Interact Club and have since risen to become its president. My experience through community service with Interact and our sponsoring Rotary club have created lasting impressions on me as well as helped to form my character. Of all my experiences of the last four years none has impacted me so much as four hours with this three-year-old.

Our sponsoring Rotary club, Carlsbad Hi-Noon, helps sponsor El Faro; a facility in Tijuana loosely called an orphanage. It is one of many facilities in the city that attempt to care for abandoned children of all ages. Some eighty children aging from three months to about fourteen years live at the facility, run by only a handful of adults. Some of the children have been at the orphanage for their entire lives.

Once a month members of the Rotary club travel to El Faro bringing food and other supplies. Recently, I had the opportunity to go with them. Spending that day at El Faro really enlightened my view of the world outside of my hometown. I have grown up in a middle class family, spending all of my life in Carlsbad, only a few miles away from the beautiful beach. My life, although not extravagant, has certainly been privileged. Like most people I had always yearned for things growing up. Perhaps a bigger house, the opportunity to travel or that new toy or outfit my friend had, but seeing children who wanted nothing more out of life than someone to hold them was a completely humbling experience. Compared to little Jorge and the children at El Faro I was rich. Eighty of them shared a facility just barely bigger than the house I now share with only my parents. The incessant hugs I receive daily from my mother would mean so much to one of those children.

I have always been aware of the millions of people in this world who are less fortunate than I but the problem always seemed too large for me to really help. At El Faro alone there are eighty children, and seventeen other such facilities in Tijuana. That is an enormous amount of people in one city alone not even considering the other numerous cities and countries around the world, many that are in much worse shape than T.J. After seeing the poverty first hand I was extremely sad and discouraged. I felt so hopeless. I thought that if I couldn't even help children that lived just an hour away from me, how could I make a difference with the other millions of people around the world? I couldn't. It just isn't possible to help them all. But then I realized something. Perhaps it is an obvious thought, but to me it bears great tangible meaning—even if I could only help one child, that was a start, a beginning. I could make a difference. No matter how small it seemed overall, I could do something that could mean wonders to one child.

In comparison to the children of Mexico I am a millionaire. The luxuries I enjoy in everyday life are things they may never have. I appreciated then the great opportunities I have to make choices and lead a successful life, the education I have at my fingertips, and the wonderful country I am so glad to live in. Although I had always been thankful for such things in my life, this experience caused me to be even more appreciative of them.

I left the orphanage with a great desire and motivation to make a difference—

any difference—no matter how small it may seem. I try to reach for my goals, both long-term and immediate, and I am eager to take advantage of the wonderful opportunities presented to me every day. I was also motivated to appreciate the things around me and the life I am so very blessed to live, and the many things I possess that others would love to have. What I learned by looking into the eyes of the three-year-old boy has been just as significant—if not more—than much of the of the "book" knowledge I have previously gained. I also have learned that people and relationships as well as experiences often teach more than a lecture ever could. This experience helped me to establish a very complex view that I treat as a *law of life*. I try to remember all that this experience has taught me and use it to help me to lead a better life, both by helping others and being more aware of the wonderful things I have. It is a complex "law" that I cannot sum up in a sentence, it is more of a view, an approach, or an awareness that I attempt to make an integral part of my daily life.

Jessica enjoys working with the Carlsbad Hi-Noon Rotary Club as a student volunteer. She plans to attend the University of California, Santa Barbara. Jessica shares that "The experience I wrote about in my essay had a profound impact on my life, and it means a lot to me that I can share this experience with others."

⌒

JOSEPH FAMILY FOUNDATION *LAWS OF LIFE* **ESSAY CONTESTS**
See profile on p. 136

Alexander Sorenson
age 17

Joseph Family Foundation
Laws of Life Essay Contests
SOUTHERN CALIFORNIA

on FAMILY
"A kind and loving family"

SINCE BIRTH I have been nurtured by a kind and loving family. My mother and father are stern but never irrational and I have a close relationship with all of my siblings. Due to this, I have not been subjected to some of the hardships of growing up that someone with a divided family may have had to deal with. I have also not been pampered and spoiled.

My father, after departing Denmark at age 17 to come to America, worked his way through college and medical school, and paid off debt for several years thereafter. He has firm values and has helped to instill them in me. My mother, who is a housewife, has spent thirty years as a full time mother. First she raised my older brother and sister and now she has almost completed raising me and my little 15-year-old sister. Another person extremely dear to my heart is my older brother Tarek, who is now 29 years old. From the moment I was conscious of having a big brother he became my supreme hero. I looked upon him with absolute, untainted admiration and he returned this love with equal compassion and vigor. As is evident by our relationship, my brother is a tender-hearted guy with a generous and lenient nature. These three prominent people in my life have helped to shape and mold me into who I am, and have aided me to define my values and beliefs.

My father took a job as a doctor in the Navy because it would allow him to spend more time with his family and not be utterly entangled with his job. During the time I have spent with him, which is considerable, several values have been seeded and nurtured to maturity. A value that has aided me in all of my endeavors is my strong work ethic; I always try to exceed expectations on all the tasks that

I attempt. My father is the person who never let me settle for mediocrity. When we would go hiking or bicycling in the countryside just outside my mother's hometown in Spain I would often want to turn back at the first sign of fatigue, but my father would say, "Let's not let the mountain defeat us," and we would both press on to the top of the hill that we were climbing and be rewarded for our efforts with a breathtaking view of the beautiful Spanish countryside.

I have a deep love for my mother. To me, she embodies morality. Every day of her life has been lived with honesty. I seriously doubt whether my mother has ever lied to me, and people learn by example. My mother will tell the truth even if it stings a little. Her truthfulness has made it unthinkable for me to lie to her. If I am ever on the verge I think how wrong it would be to lie to a mother who does not lie to me. Before I even began kindergarten this value was imbedded in my character and it has only been strengthened by my mother's and my reciprocal honesty.

My brother, who is my true hero, is a full eleven years older than I am. By the time I was three my brother had already turned fourteen and was in his teenage years when all most teenagers want to do is hang out with friends and be cool. Most older brothers in Tarek's situation couldn't have cared less about their younger siblings, but Tarek made time for both me and my little sister. When we were living in Bethesda, Maryland and I was about six years old we would go to the mall or the movies together or sometimes just walk around downtown Washington, DC. Often, what we were doing didn't matter nearly as much as just being able to spend time with a big brother that I looked up to and loved.

The large portions of time that my brother took to spend with me, and my ecstatic happiness during his presence, led me to understand how generosity and kindheartedness can bring such joy and pleasure to life, whether the giver is a family member, a friend, or a complete stranger and whether the gift is tangible or not. During the past four years I have tried to spend as much time as possible with my younger sister, and we have consequently grown very close.

Values are essential elements of anyone's life. Without them existence would be bitter and immoral and couldn't really be considered life, only existence. Once I am out from under the wing of my family I hope to maintain and even further solidify my values which will come to represent who I am and what I stand for. Eventually, I hope to be able to pass on my values to my children in the same nurturing environment in which I was raised.

Alexander has received the National Hispanic Recognition Award, the Xerox Humanities and Social Sciences Award, and the Bank of America Achievement Award. He plans to attend the University of California, Berkeley. Alexander adds that "It was gratifying to be able to pay tribute to my family in an essay that was straight from the heart."

JOSEPH FAMILY FOUNDATION *LAWS OF LIFE* ESSAY CONTESTS
See profile on p. 136

Desiree Eroy-Reveles
age 15

Joseph Family Foundation
Laws of Life Essay Contests
SOUTHERN CALIFORNIA

on HAVING FAITH
"Nothing great was ever achieved without faith"

I AM CONVINCED that the most important law in my life is to have faith: faith in God, faith in my family, faith in humanity, and most of all faith in myself. With faith great things happen. Faith brings love, trust, and confidence in my life. To lose faith is to feel lost and alone. To have faith is to believe that I have a purpose and that I can achieve.

I have faith in God. Having faith in God is very important to me, because good things happen if you believe. For example, when I was little my mom and I were in a car accident. We were pinned in our car while it was going across the highway and into a deep ditch. I prayed and the car stopped short of the ditch. I prayed that my mom was okay because the car crashed on her side. She was okay though she injured her leg and was in a wheelchair for a few months. I felt so alone and unable to help myself or my mom. However, God sent us an angel. I saw my babysitter coming toward our wreck. I was so thankful to God that she was there to take care of me and my sisters while my mom was taken to the hospital. Faith in God gave me the courage to believe that everything would be okay. Faith in God makes you feel brave even though the situation might be very scary. Having faith in God gives me guidance to go beyond my normal limits.

I have faith in my family. To have faith in my family is to have an army to fight for you. My mother, sisters, cousins, stepfather, aunts, uncles, and grandmother all are there for me. As a family, I can count on all of them to help me make it through the rough times. We are strong because we are together. When I was a baby my father left our family and this was very difficult for everyone. We all learned to accept the situation. Instead of being depressed and feeling sorry for ourselves, my mother went to school to become a bilingual teacher; both of my sisters had to become very responsible at a young age to take care of me and themselves. I have much respect and love for my family. My faith in them grows stronger each day because they help me so much!

I have faith in humanity. I have faith that justice will be done though the world is full of violence and misunderstanding. I have faith that our world will find harmony and seek peaceful resolutions. The Moslems and Jewish people are trying to have peace as neighbors. Though my high school is very racially mixed, we try to respect each others' differences and become one Oceanside family. I love the ethnic groups and how we learn about customs and cultures. I have faith that the human race will realize that life is precious and that war does not solve problems.

I have faith in myself. I believe that if I put my mind to do something, pray for God's guidance, and work very hard for what I really want, I can reach that goal. Recently I failed my biology class. My mother said that I would have to give up my dance practices to study more. I convinced her and my counselor, who wanted to put me in a general science class, that I would work harder and improve my grade. So after concentrating more on biology and making time for studying, I have brought my grade up to a B. If I did not have faith in myself I would have taken the easier class, but I stayed in biology. Now, I want to improve all my grades so that I can take tennis classes in the summer. I have faith in myself that I can put more time in my studies. I will work harder so I can do better in my grades. I have faith in myself so I know I can accomplish my goals.

Having faith is the most important law in my life. Faith in God, faith in family, faith in humanity and faith in myself will lead me to a good future. Nothing great was ever achieved without faith. As the old song goes:

Have faith, Our motto is... have faith, and you won't miss
a life of HAPPINESS when you're young remember... HAVE FAITH!!!

Desiree plans to attend college and travel as well. "Writing this essay was a very challenging experience in searching for my true values and beliefs," she shares. "There were many ways to approach it, but like my life I tried to make it simple, but meaningful."

⌒

JOSEPH FAMILY FOUNDATION *LAWS OF LIFE* ESSAY CONTESTS
See profile on p. 136

Monique Jones
age 16

Joseph Family Foundation
Laws of Life Essay Contests

SOUTHERN CALIFORNIA

on COURAGE
"The essential life quality"

To LIVE A LIFE WITH COURAGE is to live a life of gain. Courage should be a *law of life*, an essential living tool. It gives people a chance to live, not in fear, but with confidence. To live a life such as this is no doubt a tremendous gain. One gains self-confidence, happiness, and the will to continue on even when left all alone. Courage would bring out the good qualities that are sometimes hidden when left out of the light. The history of this world has proven that without courage, society would not have come as far as it has.

Courage was the main element in our world's history. Past events have shown how the use and lack of courage can either help or hurt a society. One example is the Civil Rights movement; it took courage to participate in this, and it took courage for it to succeed. All personal fears were set aside so that better lives for future generations could be achieved. Obstacles were overcome as well as goals accomplished, all because some people decided to use courage to correct what was wrong. Without a courageous foundation, all actions taken during the Civil Rights movement would have ended in failure.

However, in events such as the Holocaust, courage was an ingredient that was definitely missing. Many people died because not too many took the steps to be courageous and fight the reason that caused all those deaths. Courage surely would have been needed in order to carry out, successfully, the task of fighting for these lives. I believe that if more people had taken the path of using courage to stand against the Holocaust, sooner, many more lives would have been saved. This lack of courage has left a scar on all humanity. If courage had been a life-abiding law, this painful historic event could have been prevented much sooner. Courage is an important factor in overcoming roadblocks. It provides a person with a sense of confidence that only makes them harder to defeat. Events in history have truly shown the effects of having or lacking courage as a life tool.

Courage is an important factor in life, yet, so many times overlooked. Without courage, America might still be New England, African Americans might still be slaves, or the Holocaust still continuing on. The many liberties we have access to are often taken for granted. Sometimes people forget that their freedom or human rights were not acquired gradually or by chance. Many times it took pain and suffering to attain them. Due to the courage of past forefathers, lives today are much happier. We should not overlook the importance of having courage in our lives. It took courage for this world to accomplish its many goals and succeed because of it. I strive to live my life with courage and only hope that other people will do the same. Courage not only gives materialistic rewards, but also a personal feeling of accomplishment. It's an unexplainable feeling that can't come from worldly or man-made treasures. It is a quality that is well earned, and once gained, can never be taken away by anyone.

Monique enjoys reading, singing, and playing the piano. She hopes to graduate from high school with honors and study pre-law in college. By writing a laws of life *essay, Monique believes that she was able to "overcome my fear of not being good enough to succeed."*

⌒

JOSEPH FAMILY FOUNDATION *LAWS OF LIFE* ESSAY CONTESTS
See profile on p. 136

Nadine Bastiampillai
age 15

Turning Points Program
ONTARIO, CANADA

on LIVING LIFE TO THE FULLEST
"My turning point"

WHEN I WAS FIRST GIVEN this assignment I did not know what to write about. As I looked back on my life, I realized that there was only one thing I could write about, my granduncle's death. I chose this subject because it has helped me look at life from a different perspective.

I have never had a grandfather. My mother's father died when she was eight, and she doesn't really talk about him because it is too painful. My father's dad died at the age of 33 of a heart attack. My father is not the type of person to show his emotions, so he also doesn't talk about his father. He was 13 years old when his father died. My dad's uncle took him and his brothers in, while our grandmother worked in another country to make money so she could send it to them so that they could have a good life. My granduncle has been like a father to my dad, and a grandfather to me. We'd visit him as a family when we were young, but as we grew older we stopped visiting as often, then finally, we all stopped visiting him altogether. We thought he would always be there.

Then one day last year we got a call from my grandmother telling us that my granduncle was in the hospital. He had a stroke and was in a coma. My dad immediately left the house to see him in the hospital. When we got there my cousins, aunts, and uncles were already there. My aunt told the children that he was alright and that he would be out soon. But after a month, he was still in the hospital. My family and I would visit him as often as we could. Then one day when my grandmother and I were at the hospital, he came out of his coma. Our entire family was happy! He started talking. We all thought that he was going to make it out of the hospital. Then on Wednesday, March 10, 1999, we received a call from a family member saying that he had died in his sleep.

When my father first found out, he didn't cry or show any sign of emotion. When the funeral came around, we all went. The sermon was beautiful. Afterwards, we took turns going to the coffin to say our good-byes. I saw my father go up to the coffin, hold my granduncle's hand and cry. For the first time in my life, I saw my father cry. For as long as I've known him, I have never seen him shed a tear. That's when I realized I would never see my granduncle again.

My granduncle's death helped me to realize that death happens to everyone. Through this painful experience I have learned to live each and every day, and never hold back because you never know if you can have the same opportunity again. I regret not visiting my "grandfather" before his stroke, but I pray to him every day. I know that he is in heaven right now, looking down on me.

Nadine enjoys traveling and is spending part of her summer touring England, Scotland, and France. During the school year, she is an active volunteer at a local shelter. Nadine hopes to pursue a degree in mathematics.

TURNING POINTS PROGRAM

After hearing about the essay contest from Sir John Templeton, senior executives at Fairfax Financial Holdings Limited, a financial services company, decided to bring the program to Canada and establish a significant contest throughout the province of Ontario. The challenge for both Fairfax and the John Templeton Foundation was to find a high caliber organization capable of administering a successful, large-scale contest.

After an extensive search, the choice was clear: The Learning Partnership, a Toronto-based, non-profit educational organization that brings together business and education leaders to design and implement effective school programs, would be an ideal "home" for the contest. The Learning Partnership immediately identified with the ideals of the contest and is now working to implement the contest throughout Ontario.

The Learning Partnership has named the contest "Turning Points," and this past spring, the contest was launched as a pilot program to both French and English-speaking students in Toronto-area high schools. The contest has been well received by teachers as an effective learning program that contributes to the Literacy Outcomes of the Ontario Curriculum. Plans are underway to launch the contest throughout the Province of Ontario, and the groundwork is being laid to expand the contest across Canada.

Lori Cranson, Vice President of The Learning Partnership, is delighted to be involved in the program: "We want to thank Fairfax Financial for making the contest possible in Ontario. The *Turning Points* Program will have an impact on the choices our young people make and how they will live their lives." ✳

Malieka Overton
age 13

Northwestern Middle School
Laws of Life Essay Contest

ALBION, PENNSYLVANIA

on RESPECT
"Respecting other people can make a difference"

WHEN I WAS LITTLE, I used to think the world was perfect and that everybody was happy. I thought that everybody loved each other. Lately, I've come to find that I was wrong. Some people are kind and generous, while others are not. I am an African American in the seventh grade and lately I've been dealing with a problem. There is a boy in my class who always makes racial comments toward me. I don't think he thinks about what he says before he says it. I don't think he knows that he can hurt people's feelings, or maybe he does. I've always let it slide, but it's getting old. He says that he's just joking, but I know he isn't sometimes. He constantly says that black people are annoying. I don't know how many black people he has met, but it's not enough to judge all African Americans.

At times I think to myself, even if he is joking, would he like me to call him names and talk about him just because of the color of his skin? Would he like me to make jokes about him hanging from a tree? I don't think he would. I don't think he means any harm, but he has done it one too many times. It's not so much that it bothers me, it's just that if he doesn't learn to respect other people and their feelings, he could get himself in a lot of trouble and also hurt a lot of people in the process.

This is just one of my stories of how courtesy and respect can make a difference. If that boy just happens to read this story, he'll know what he's done. I hope he realizes his problem and makes the change. If everybody showed some respect for one another, maybe the world would be a happier place. Just remember, it doesn't matter who you are, or where you are, you don't have to like a person to be respectful and be courteous.

Malieka plans to attend college. She enjoys playing basketball, softball, and the saxo-phone.

NORTHWESTERN MIDDLE SCHOOL *LAWS OF LIFE* ESSAY CONTEST

"When I first heard about this incredible essay contest from the Center for Youth Issues (CYI)," says school guidance counselor Virginia Sampson, "I was determined to bring the contest to Northwestern Middle School."

Thanks to Ms. Sampson's determination and support from CYI, over 250 Northwestern students participated in the contest this past year. The Northwestern school district and Country Greens, a local business, sponsored the new contest.

"The contest has a promising future at Northwestern Middle School," says Ms. Sampson. "Students need this opportunity to share their thoughts and life learning experiences." ✳

Kati Lestmann
age 17

Rhea County
Character Education Contest

RHEA COUNTY, TENNESSEE

on LIVING BY YOUR VALUES
"The train to attain character"

CHARACTER, or moral excellence and firmness, is a virtue that is not instinctive. It takes hard work and is made up of many different attributes. Character is something that has to be learned through many life lessons. It can be thought of as a train on its way to a destination. You start out with an engine, or the decision to *want* to have character. The attainment of character is yours and the train's destination. In between the start and the finish are many stops. These stops are trials that help you acquire a new trait, or a new car, to add to the train of character.

At one train stop, you will have to learn respect, both for yourself and everyone else. You have to choose the paths in life that will have the most positive effects. You must show high regard for others and value them as yourself. When you have picked up the ability to treat everyone equally, you will be on your way again.

The next car you will pick up is responsibility. This car is a little bit more difficult to pick up because it means you will have to remember your promises and abide by them. Responsibility will show most through your actions, so you must be careful of which tracks you commit to.

From there, you will go straight to perseverance. Hard work is mostly required for this part of your train. You will battle many hills, and you will have to push with all of your heart- and mind-strength to overcome them. Proper determination can help, but you all will also need a good dose of patience. It might take a little bit longer to achieve this trait, but you will learn it. Just hanging in there is the best advice for this car.

Right on down the rail a way is caring. This should be a little bit easier for you, since you've already had a load of it picked up when you added respect to your train. However, you will still have to think before you act. Making sure to listen when others need an open ear is necessary, as well as the willingness to put others' needs and personal interests above your own. You must be willing to forgive any wrongs that may be done against you. With that, caring will be added and you'll start chugging away.

Self-discipline is the next stop, and this is another big load of learning to pull. This car makes sure you can handle all you've loaded yourself down with. It weeds out the unnecessary baggage and keeps the good. It shows good control over the direction your train is headed in.

By now you are on your second half of the journey. The stop in citizenship is next, but it should be a quick one. It is here that you will learn to obey the law. You will also help out in your community as much as possible by donating your time and efforts to worthy causes.

As you near the next pick-up, you begin to wonder if you will ever reach your destination. You think about taking some short cuts that you've heard of from others who have followed the same path, but you notice that they have something missing. This "something" is honesty, or being true to yourself and others. By taking the easy way out, they failed to learn a very important lesson. This will affect them on all of their other journeys in life. You attain honesty quite quickly, since you already showed that you have integrity by following the rules and choosing the right path.

Perseverance will play hand in hand with the next link in the chain: courage. This attribute takes guts to add to your train. It says that you are willing to rise above the usual and face a challenge head on. It will take perseverance, since this car has a little bit more weight to it than the others, but you'll succeed due to your self-discipline.

Light of heart, and feeling light of load, you make your final stop at fairness. This characteristic proves how much respect for yourself and the law you really have. You prove that you will make right and just decisions based on all the facts given, regardless of whether the outcome will hurt you most in the end. You risk being ridiculed and despised for making wise decisions, but you know that you'll come out better in the end for it.

Having attained all of the necessary traits, you head on to your final destination: character. It's not very far, for once you've mastered respect, responsibility, perseverance, caring, self-discipline, citizenship, honesty, courage, and fairness, you've already gotten character. It's just a matter of putting it into practice in your every-day lifestyle.

Just over the top of the next hill, you see the city of character. Everyone who has preceded you on this path is there, cheering you on at the top of his or her lungs. They eagerly await your train, knowing very well that what you have for them will benefit everyone.

As you slow down, you realize that your journey has really just begun. You are not discouraged, though, for you know that from here on out it will be much easier, since you are done with your training to attain character. You have what it takes to be successful on all tracks of life.

Kati has won numerous awards, including a full scholarship to Bryan College. She adds that "Writing a laws of life *essay served as a good reminder for me of what it takes to have true character."*

⌒

RHEA COUNTY CHARACTER EDUCATION CONTEST

What can make a strawberry festival that much sweeter? How about $1,550 in prizes! The essay contest was launched this past year in Rhea County, Tennessee, in conjunction with the annual Dayton Chamber of Commerce Strawberry Festival. The contest is sponsored by Bryan College, the *Herald News*, and the Center for Youth Issues.

The Strawberry Festival is helping to promote positive character in Rhea County by starting a coloring and a poster character education contest, as well as the *Laws of Life* Essay Contest. Schools participating in the essay contest include Rhea Central Elementary, Spring City Elementary School, and Rhea County High School.

The contest's first awards ceremony was held at the Strawberry Festival and included a performance by STARS (Students Taking a Right Stand). At the ceremony, six student prizewinners and their teachers received a total of $1,200 in awards for their participation in the contest.

Dr. William E. Brown, president of Bryan College, explains why the college got behind the contest: "We helped to sponsor and coordinate the contest because we believe the building of character is a fundamental part of a true education. We are so pleased to help our local schools by providing this dynamic character education program." ✳

Gloria Kung
age 15

Georgia *Laws of Life* Essay Contest
ATLANTA, GEORGIA

on LOVE
"The power of love"

WHAT EXACTLY IS LOVE? You hear people talking about it all the time, but do you know what it is? Do you know how love can change one's life tremendously? When I was in sixth grade, I had just moved to the United States from Taiwan, an island east of China. The new foreign land was so unfamiliar to me, and I was mad at the world, I was angry at my mother for taking me out of my homeland, I was angry at the people around me who have friends and the happy and carefree lives of theirs. I felt lonely and helpless. There was no way for me to make friends due to my lack of knowledge in English. My grades were dropping in school, because I couldn't understand anything that my teachers were teaching. I felt frustrated and useless. All the glories that I had back in Taiwan were all buried underground, with nobody to share them with. I felt as if somebody was choking me, and I couldn't talk, move, or even breathe. I was slowly dying inside and threw the thought of me having a bright future away.

Fortunately, just as I was about to give up all my hopes, I met my new English teacher. At first I was intimidated by her because of all the stories that I have heard from her previous students. I walked into her classroom the first day with my legs trembling, unable to stay calm. She greeted me with the big, friendly smile of hers and talked to me. After a few sentences, she realized that I could not speak English well. That was when she said something that no teacher had said to me before, and supplied oxygen for my dying flame inside. She promised me that I would be just like any other kids in my school when I finished with her class. She assured me of my success in the future and the happiness that I would experience. I became a little more confident as I sat down in my seat.

Her name is Mrs. Mayerchak. She has a passion for her job and cares for all of her students. She taught us the importance to strive for excellence at all times, and she taught us to be kind and loving. On the first day of class, she made me walk around the classroom to talk with my fellow classmates. Surprisingly, the people that I feared so much greeted me with welcoming smiles and warm embraces that filled my heart. From that point on, I opened up more and stopped hating the world. Meanwhile, Mrs. Mayerchak patiently taught me the different techniques of the English language. She used her own hard-earned money to hire a tutor to explain things for me during school. She would stay after school to go over my work and teach me vocabulary. She would also interest me with movies that motivated me to speak English fluently. In addition, she would bring in music and keep the English language appealing.

Furthermore, Mrs. Mayerchak didn't just stop there. She would call or come to my house once in a while just to teach me some more English and talk to me without charging. She would go out of her way just to make sure that I grasped all the materials. She became my best friend who supported me through all my decisions and helped me in every situation. I felt a kind of love that touched me deep within my heart. Because of her endless caring and assistance, my grades were getting better and better and I made friends. I talked more and more each day, and the fear of being different and lonely slowly faded away. I am now a talkative girl with friends. My grades are good and my life is going well. I am now part of the American world, a place that was once frightening and strange, thanks to the time and thoughtfulness of Mrs. Mayerchak. Because of the love that she has given me, I feel accepted and at home. I will never ever forget what she had done for me.

From this experience of mine, I would conclude that love is one of the most important *laws of life*. It is out of love that people have the courage to help somebody and do tasks that are tough. From love comes the kindness and caring that make the world a better place. By being loving, you can make somebody smile, and the cheerfulness of that person can pass on to others. It is out of love that generosity came and the need to be fair grows. From love there comes patience and respect. So many characters that are desired in life spring from love. Love can make you everything people ask of you. What would the world be like without love? Will we be able to endure our lives without feeling loved?

Gloria plans to attend either Berkeley or Stanford University and hopes to become a news anchor or reporter. "Writing my laws of life *essay has made me appreciate the little things in life," she shares. "I realize that everything we do is for a purpose, either for ourselves or for others. This essay made me realize that the world is not full of evil-doers —there are still people who care."*

~

GEORGIA *LAWS OF LIFE* ESSAY CONTEST

"I am glad to sponsor such a worthwhile program, one that encourages students to articulate their beliefs," says J.B. Fuqua, contest sponsor and well-known Atlanta businessman and philanthropist.

The Georgia Contest began in the spring of 2000, and in its very first year 15 Greater Atlanta Metro Area schools participated in the contest. The contest has been enthusiastically endorsed as an important character education program by the Georgia Department of Education, the Georgia Humanities Council, and the Georgia Center for Character Education.

In the spring of 2000, more than 6,000 Georgia students wrote a *laws of life* essay. At an awards dinner held at the Atlanta Ritz Carlton, the winning essayists received over $4,500 in cash prizes. Emory University served as the contest's fiscal agent, and the university's work-study students participated in the essay screening process.

Amy Butler, director of the Georgia Essay Contest, had previously helped to establish a successful contest in Palm Beach County, Florida. "Helping young people learn what matters most is what the contest is all about," says Ms. Butler. "That's why when I moved to Atlanta I knew I had to start a contest for the students of Georgia." ✳

Victoria Kintner
age 18

Shreveport *Laws of Life* Essay Contest
SHREVEPORT, LOUISIANA

on LIVING LIFE SIMPLY
"I experienced giving with the hands of God"

I HAD MY SUITCASES PACKED, complete with reading material to fight off boredom and Cheez balls to ward off hunger. I was excited and raring to go. In my mind, I was completely prepared for my trip to Mexico. Now I realize I was anything but ready.

My heart was beating so quickly it hurt. My palms were sweaty. Anxiety overwhelmed my entire body. I thought it was just the nervousness of crossing into a foreign country, but even after we had crossed the border, it didn't stop. I began second-guessing my strength and preparedness, both physically and spiritually, for this journey. As we drove through the little town of Rio Bravo, my mind could not comprehend all that my eyes were seeing. I saw children with no shoes, in little more than their underwear, running through rocky, dirty roads. Crowded on every street were shacks of plywood and sheet metal in which families of six lived a cramped existence. Threadbare sheets were used for doors. It seemed as though the small homes would topple with the slightest wind. I shuddered at the thought of children enduring cold and inclement weather with little or no shelter. Emaciated dogs, with only patches of fur left on their bony bodies, ate scraps out of trash piles. I didn't know what to think. Mexico was run-down, dirty, and destitute: I had crossed out of my comfort zone.

At first I felt helpless. I doubted that our contribution would make the tiniest difference in their lives. How could a small cinder-block home even begin to solve their problems? Ironically, I had come to give to them, and yet I was to be the one who would receive the most.

I live in a world of consumerism and materialism. There is never enough and it never happens quickly enough. I struggle with being content with my financial standings and social status. I often let the opinions of others control my life. Greed and selfishness frequently overcome me. The people of Rio Bravo gave me a new perspective. I was intrigued by their simple way of life. They didn't live in my fast-paced, "got-to achieve-more" world. Worries did not bog them down. Relaxation came easily to them. I am sure they faced hardships, but when they did they saw opportunity. They lived the life I knew only in my dreams. Although engulfed in poverty, everyone I met was rich in spirit. I could feel the atmosphere of intimacy and support. They were amazing, they were humble, they were beautiful.

My group, *the constructores de fe,* or faith builders, constructed a home for a family of four. There was a young mother of eighteen with sparkling black eyes, and her two young children, ages four and six months. Eva, the four-year-old, had the most mischievous eyes. Any time I looked at her she would smile and run off giggling as if she knew something I didn't. The baby, whose name I couldn't pronounce, simply slept in her mother's arms as she rocked in an old, white rocking chair. Because I had injured my leg on the first day, I was given the job of playing with the numerous neighborhood children. What had seemed misfortune soon became a great blessing. We talked and danced. We played soccer and Red-Rover. We drew pictures and blew bubbles. We gave gifts and exchanged smiles. Our language barriers crumbled at the sound of laughter and the sight of love. In just three short days, we became the best of friends. I still cry when I picture their beautiful faces and little feet running after the van on the last day.

Through this mission trip, I learned that in order to be exposed to a new culture, I must allow myself to be open and vulnerable. I experienced giving with the hands of God, expecting nothing in return. I became more appreciative of my life, not only of my material possessions, but of the unconditional love that embraces me. I know that we provided them with a new home, a new broom, and even some toys for the children, temporary things at best. What they gave me was precious and enduring, the hope and desire for a simple life.

"Not so with you. Instead, whoever wants to be great among you must be a servant, and whoever wants to be first must be slave of all." —Mark 10:43–44

Victoria would like to become a speech pathologist and work with children. "Writing this essay helped me fully realize what my trip to Mexico taught me," she explains. "I learned that a piece of writing is never completely finished—something can always be improved."

SHREVEPORT *LAWS OF LIFE* ESSAY CONTEST

This past year the Wilcox Foundation and Centenary College of Louisiana came together to sponsor an essay contest in Shreveport, Louisiana. Centenary, a small, private liberal arts college, recently celebrated 175 years of academic excellence and in 1999 was included in *U.S. News & World Report* as the "No. 1 Best Value" among the South's colleges and universities.

The college felt that the contest was a wonderful way to reach the young people in the surrounding community of Caddo Parish. Invitations and encouragement to participate were extended to all high school English teachers. An intimate and elegant awards reception was held at the college, and included the announcement of the top three winners who were awarded partial scholarships to Centenary College.

The Wilcox Foundation shares Centenary College's enthusiasm for the essay contest, because the contest helps meet one of the Foundation's major objectives: Enriching educational and character building opportunities for high school and college students. ✴

Anna Kopel
age 14

Mankato *Laws of Life* Essay Contest
MANKATO, MINNESOTA

on PERSEVERANCE
"What I learned from my grandmother"

TWO YEARS AGO, my grandma left this earth. It wasn't until after she died that I truly recognized how much she actually meant to me. She was my friend, my teacher, my inspiration. She taught me things that became my own personal *laws of life*. They are lessons that have helped me get through each day with a smile. They are lessons that have made me aware of my strong points as well as my weaknesses, and helped me to overcome those weaknesses. They are true lessons to live by, and I hope I will never forget them.

One day, my grandma told me something I will always remember. She said: "Your talent is God's gift to you. What you do with it is your gift to God."

Those words have somewhat become a part of me over the years. Each day I thank God for the many talents He has given me, and I try to use those talents in a way which helps me grow closer to Him. I believe that we were all born to reveal the glory of God that is within us. It's not just in some of us, it is in everyone. And as we each let our own light shine, through our talents and ideas, we unconsciously give others permission to do the same. Just think about what our world could be like if each and every one of us let our own light shine through. I think our world would be a much better place, growing together the way God intended.

One more lesson my grandma taught me was to always go for my dreams and never, ever give up. She once told me: "Shoot for the moon, because even if you fall, you'll land among the stars."

I have never heard anything more true in all my life. I have tried to live by these words, and have figured out that it is very important to go for your dreams and never let anything get in your way. Even if you have had a bad experience in the past, never limit your view of life by that experience. I believe that life is constantly testing our level of commitment, and I am convinced life's greatest rewards are reserved for those who show a never-ending commitment to act until they achieve. This level of determination can accomplish amazing things, but it must be continual and consistent. As simple as this may sound, it is still the common denominator separating those who live their dreams from those that live in regret.

Another great lesson my grandma taught me was: "Never let anyone come to you without coming away better and happier." Everyone should see goodness in your face, in your eyes, in your smile. Too often we underestimate the power of such things: a touch, a smile, a kind word, a listening ear, an honest compliment, or even the smallest act of caring. All have the potential to turn a life around. We should welcome everyone as we would welcome Christ Himself, because He is a part of each and every one of us.

My grandma is no longer present here on earth, but she will always remain present in my heart. Her words and personality have affected my life in ways I never thought possible. Her lessons on life have become a part of me, and have made me a better person. I will never forget the great love my grandma shared with everyone, her great faith in God, or her inspirational words. She is my idol. My grandma's *laws of life* will live in me forever.

Anna has won numerous art, science, and math awards. She would like to pursue a career in business, medicine, or architecture. Anna adds that "I hope my essay will help others to dig deep within themselves to find their special talent, and once they've found it, to live it out, because the value of their life depends on it."

⤳

MANKATO *LAWS OF LIFE* ESSAY CONTEST

When semi-retired insurance and investment broker Carl Schoenstedt was reading Sir John Templeton's book, *Discovering the Laws of Life*, he came upon Sir John's description of the essay contest. As Mr. Schoenstedt explains, "I immediately realized that the contest could make a difference in young people's lives right here in Mankato, Minnesota." With the help of local educators Jane Schuck, Kevin Hulke and Jim Rouse, he promoted the contest to Mankato schools, churches, businesses, and the local media.

Thanks to Mr. Schoenstedt's efforts, thirty-six community sponsors, including many local businesses and individuals, sponsored the first Mankato Contest in the spring of 2000. The sponsors include: John and Vonis Behrends, John and Aileen Bipes, Charles and Virginia Danish, Preston Doyle, Richard and Nancy Hamer, John and Ann Heimark, John and Cynthia Hoines, Ellis and Jane Jones, Leroy and Anita Jordan, Don Kvasnicka, Carl and Rita Schoenstedt, Austin Auto Repair, Inc., Burger King of Mankato, Dakota Meadows PTO, East High School PTO, the *Free Press*, Hardee's, HickoryTech, Hy-Vee, Immanuel Lutheran School PTO, Kitchenmaster and Co., KTOE and KDOG, Mankato Sertoma, Maschka, Riedy & Ries Law Firm, Northern Star Bank, Presbyterian Church, Quality 1 Hour Foto, River Hills Mall, Sign Pro, Southern Minnesota Construction, Subway, US Bancorp Piper Jaffray, Wells Fargo Bank, and Z-99 Radio.

Students from eight area schools, both public and private, participated in the contest: Fitzgerald Middle School, Dakota Meadows Middle School, East Junior High School, East High School, Mankato West High School, Mankato East High School, Loyola High School, and Immanuel Lutheran School. Bethlehem Lutheran Church donated its reception hall for the awards ceremony. Ten middle school students won cash prizes totaling $2,000, and with the administrative support of Frank Brandt, president of the Mankato Chapter of Dollars for Scholars, ten high school students were awarded higher education scholarships totaling $3,000.

Way to go, Mankato! ✳

Kevin Holloway
age 20

CHARACTER*plus*
Laws of Life Essay Contest

ST. LOUIS, MISSOURI

on PATIENCE
"Getting past the potholes of life"

WHEN I WAS growing up in St. Louis, my mother and father stressed to me that in order to succeed in life you must have patience. Take your time and observe all things, they said. I wish I had listened to what my mother and father said about patience. Without patience you pass up so many opportunities in life!

I wish that I had practiced patience. I used to race through life like a thief in the night without stopping to think of the dangers or consequences of my actions. It's like I was leaping into the ocean without knowing its depth. It's times like that that I wished I were like a deer frozen in a car's headlights. Then I would have had at least a moment to think about what to do.

I learned that patience is something you must have because in 1997 I didn't have the patience to stay in school and finish. I was so in a rush to skip class and play with my friends that I let my impatience get the better of me, and I let my high school diploma fly by.

I lost my father to a heart attack in 1988. Two years later I lost my mother from a stroke. I wish now that I had taken the time to show them the love they showed me. The biggest thing I noticed was that I hadn't really paid attention to my life and I didn't realize how important the people were in my life.

After they died, I went to stay with my Auntie, and I stayed with her for two months before a custody battle began with the courts. They tried to put me into a foster home, but my Auntie fought for four straight months to keep me with her. So now, I still live with her.

Now that I have the patience to sit and learn, I see things differently. For example, I took the time to sit down and make a blueprint of the mistakes and the poor decisions that my impatience caused me over the years.

Because of that I have made the decision to return to school because I got tired of racing through life without an education. I now attend the G.E.D. program at Covenant House in St. Louis, Missouri. Each morning I take a five minute bus ride to the Metrolink, then a twenty minute ride to the Grand Station on the Metrolink, then another ten minute bus ride to get to my classes—two buses and one train to get to school each day. I come here because I like the education that Covenant House provides because the adults take the time to really sit down and help you with the potholes of your life. Now that I have the patience to sit and learn, I see things differently.

Now my goal is to get my G.E.D. and build a solid foundation for myself. Writing this paper has caused me to think about slowing down and looking at the whole perspective of my life, not focusing on the tempting things such as fancy cars, clothes, and immaterial things. Instead, I plan to focus on education, knowledge of many cultures and backgrounds, the heritage of the United States, and other important things that will help me to become a well-spoken businessman in my city.

Kevin's goal is to be a NASA engineer. He credits his teacher Nancy Saguto with helping him determine his law of life *and how to write about it. Kevin shares that "At first writing the essay didn't mean much, but as I started writing, it really brought back to me the key thing about patience."*

∽

CHARACTER*PLUS LAWS OF LIFE* ESSAY CONTEST

In the near future, 40,000 students in 68 St. Louis-area high schools will be invited to write a *laws of life* essay as part of their involvement in CHARACTER*plus,* a nationally recognized character education initiative of the St. Louis Cooperating School Districts.

This past year, the CHARACTER*plus* Contest was launched as a pilot program at Covenant House, a shelter that provides services to young adults 17 to 21 years old who have dropped out of high school and are working toward their GED. In the spring of 2000, all of the young people who participated in the program read their essays at an awards luncheon.

According to Bonnie Davis, a Covenant House volunteer who worked closely with the essay writers, "Participating in the contest provided these young people with an opportunity to reflect and re-examine how their prior decisions have had negative consequences. Now, hopefully these young men and women will begin their new lives with a greater self-awareness and sense of purpose." ✳

Margaret Therese (Terry) Bruns *age 16*

Guilford County *Laws of Life*
Creative Expressions Contest

GUILFORD COUNTY, NORTH CAROLINA

on LIVING BY YOUR VALUES
"A recipe for character"

INGREDIENTS:

One (1) strong sense of right and wrong
(May be refined over a period of years for strongest effect)

One (1) hearty sense of humor
(Should be compatible with all slips, blunders and falls to be added later)

A handful of compassion
(Should be added where seen fit, however it is impossible to add too much)

A pinch of tact (To be tossed in if ingredients appear too bitter)

A dash of failure (To help eventual success taste sweeter)

*Optional—Dozens of life experiences and feelings. Do not be afraid to experiment with sorrow, joy, envy and love.

DIRECTIONS:

Mix moral sense with a dash of failure. If flavor of moral sense prevails, move to next step. If mixture still tastes bitter, add tact and compassion until smoothly blended.
*Note: Failures add to the ultimate flavor of the recipe.
If omitted, product will be incomplete.
However, make sure to balance mixture with a strong moral sense.

Add sorrow, joy, envy and love to mixture until bowl is filled. Failure to add these will cause complications in later preparation.

PREPARATION TIME:
One (1) lifetime

YIELDS:
One (1) heaping pile of character. This can be used for various purposes, including, but not limited to: getting the most out of life, sticking up for the underdog, making safe and healthy decisions, feeling fulfilled, teaching others, learning the truth about yourself (good and bad), and having the courage to make a difference in someone's life. You will find that this recipe comes in handy particularly in times of distress and despair. If ingredients are added correctly, the essential elements of character can be served up in any situation. Then you know you have prepared a recipe not only for character, but for life as well.

Terry's goal is to one day be the editor of her own publishing house and teach English at the college level.

⁓

GUILFORD COUNTY *LAWS OF LIFE* CREATIVE EXPRESSIONS CONTEST
"A picture is worth a thousand words." The young people of Guilford County, North Carolina have proven that there are many ways to express the *laws of life*—that's because their contest includes art, music, video, and photography, as well as the written word!

Charlie Abourjilie, Coordinator of the Guilford County Character Education Council, first heard about the essay contest from Warren Romaine, who sponsors a contest in neighboring Montgomery County. Mr. Abourjilie immediately realized that the contest was a natural fit for the community of Guilford County and a great way for children to reflect upon their most important values.

Although only in its first year, a large number of local businesses and organizations have gotten involved in the contest, including: Ad Color, Carolina Bank, the Center for Youth Issues, Central Carolina Bank, Greensboro College, the Greensboro Merchants Association, the Guilford County Character Education Council, Jefferson Pilot Corporation, and VF Corporation.

In its first year, a total of 25 public and private schools participated in the Creative

Expressions Contest. At the awards ceremony held at Greensboro College, more than $9,000 in cash prizes was awarded to 24 middle and high school students. In the spirit of giving something back to their community, the winners received a second cash prize that they donated to the charity of their choice. ✳

Nicole Kuncl
age 15

Martin County *Laws of Life* Essay Contest
MARTIN COUNTY, FLORIDA

on COMPASSION
"Taking the time to smile"

THERE IS AN OLD AESOP FABLE that tells the story of a lion and a mouse. As the story goes, a mighty lion was enjoying a nap when a tiny mouse ran across his paw and wakened him. The lion was just about to make a snack of the mouse when he cried, "Please let me go. You never know, some day I might be able to help you." Of course, the lion scoffed at the idea that a little mouse would ever be of any help to a great lion. However, the lion was feeling benevolent that day, so he allowed the mouse to go. A few days later, the lion was trapped in a net. He pushed and struggled with all his might, but the ropes were too strong. He roared with frustration. The tiny mouse, not too far away, heard the lion and ran to him. With his sharp teeth, he gnawed through the ropes of the net and set the lion free. The tiny mouse truly had been able to repay the kindness of the mighty lion.

This story is a wonderful example of the virtue of compassion. Compassion can be defined as the sharing of the distress of another, and doing what one can to relieve that person's suffering. One could say compassion is almost synonymous with kindness. In the case of the lion and the mouse, it was compassion that saved the mouse from becoming a meal, for the lion showed mercy to the tiny mouse and let it go. Once again, it was compassion that inspired the mouse to come to the rescue of the trapped lion. However, compassion can take many forms, most of which are not nearly as grand as saving the life of another.

Showing compassion to another person can be very simple. Sometimes, simply smiling at someone can be an incredibly powerful gesture. For example, anywhere one goes there is almost always the guarantee that there will be someone there who is considered an outcast. The next time one sees this person, instead of ignoring him and walking on by, taking a second to smile and offer a greeting would make a world of difference. Or, perhaps there is someone one knows who is always teased, picked on and insulted. Instead of joining in on the chorus of jeers, or merely remaining a silent bystander, a wonderful compassionate gesture would be to stand up for the less fortunate person being tormented. These examples both beautifully depict how easily one can show compassion to another.

Being compassionate can make everyone's lives so much better. Simply knowing that someone cares enough to show kindness makes one's day seem brighter. In addition, if one makes it a point to be kind to others, it makes him feel better about himself. One who is compassionate knows he is sympathetic, considerate, helpful, and in short, a caring human being. Therefore, having compassion is its own reward.

Compassion is such an incredibly important *law of life* that everyone should try to live by. Kindness only takes a simple gesture, and results in a better quality of life for everyone who is touched by it. If all people made it a practice to be compassionate and kind, only think of how much happier everyone would be. Everyone would know that he or she was cared about, and all people would be able to feel that they were caring, kind human beings. Imagine, such happiness sparked by something as simple as taking the time to smile.

Nicole is very thankful to her teacher, Mrs. Leonard, for encouraging her English class to write a laws of life *essay. She adds that "I hope the message of my essay reaches people, because I think kindness truly is the most important* law of life.*"*

                                                                               ~

MARTIN COUNTY *LAWS OF LIFE* ESSAY CONTEST

Sponsor Jeff Jaffe, former CEO of numerous confectionery and food companies, heard Sir John Templeton speak about the essay contest at a Chief Executives Organization meeting. Mr. Jaffe was so impressed with the program that he decided to sponsor a contest in his community of Martin County, Florida. Soon, the local high schools, the *Stuart News,* the Martin County Board of Commissioners, and the school district were all involved in the contest.

The first Martin County Contest took place in January, 2000. Essays were submitted from two high schools and three alternative schools, including one boot camp. Thirteen finalists won over $5,000 in cash prizes, and the teacher of each winner also received a cash award. Invited guests at the awards reception included the superintendent of schools, the publisher of the *Stuart News*, county commissioners, and the mayor of Stuart.

Mr. Jaffe believes the contest is a perfect way to give something back to his community. "The opportunity to bring the contest to Martin County has provided great satisfaction to me, and I am so pleased our community and schools have welcomed the contest." ✳

Lisa Avery
age 14

Omaha *Laws of Life* Essay Contest
OMAHA, NEBRASKA

on LIVING LIFE TO THE FULLEST
"The most important part of life is life itself"

I FIRST BEGAN WRITING this paper while in Oklahoma City on the fifth anniversary of the bombing of the Alfred P. Murrah Federal Building. To start with I thought about all the good qualities I admire in people. I came up with many, but as I sat listening to the dedication ceremony of the Oklahoma City National Memorial, it became clear to me. It is not any of these wonderful characteristics that are the most important *law of life*. I realized that the most important part of life is life itself.

As I listened to the ceremony, I heard many speakers; first, a mother who lost her youngest child, then an employee who lost many co-workers and friends, and next the fire chief who helped save so many lives. The next speakers included the mayor, senator, Attorney General Janet Reno and finally the president, Bill Clinton. Death and tragedy can impact so many people and touch them all in different ways. The tragedy in Oklahoma City was felt by people all over the country. The whole country united as Americans to prove that love can overpower hatred and joy overcome sorrow. The death of a loved one is a loss that can only be understood by a person that has felt this pain. The families of the 168 victims know this feeling all too well. Nineteen of the victims were children or unborn children. There are seven to eight hundred people who survived the bombing that day. I am sure they now know how important it is to appreciate and cherish life.

On April 19, 1994, my aunt was sitting in her home about twenty miles north of downtown Oklahoma City. At 9:02 am, she felt such a vibration that she believed the house next door had exploded. My uncle, a doctor, was covering the

Emergency Room at Veteran's Hospital in downtown Oklahoma City. He helped care for many people injured in the blast, including some young children. One young girl and her mother came back to the hospital a few days after the bombing to thank my uncle for his care. I'm sure it is occasions like this that make it clear to him why he became a doctor, to help people in their time of crisis. This is also the great feeling of joy and accomplishment that makes me consider possibly having a career in the medical field.

This January I lost the last of my grandparents. The first of my grandparents to pass away was my grandpa ten years ago. His wife, my grandma, died of lung cancer three years later in 1993. My other grandma died in 1996 when I was in the fifth grade. My last grandpa passed away in January.

Grandparents are a very important part of any person's life. They are always there to help you or cheer you up when you are sad. Grandparents are around to spend holidays with, to give presents to and get presents from. Grandparents are meant to tell stories and encourage their grandchildren. Most supportive grandparents go to dance recitals, baseball games, honor banquets, basketball games, and graduations whenever they can.

When a person's grandparents pass away, a big part of their life is lost. It is hard to sit and listen to all my friends talk about going to their grandparents or all the presents their grandparents gave them for their birthday or Christmas. I know that I will never be able to experience that part of my life again. It makes me sad to go to all the baseball games and see all the grandparents sitting there cheering on their grandchildren. I also feel a sense of joy for the children whose grandparents support and encourage them in everything they do. I wish I could tell them all how lucky they are and how important it is to enjoy the special time they have with their grandparents. I would tell them to always appreciate and respect their grandparents and everything they do for them. They will never know when one of them could suddenly pass away. It is also hard for me because I have two little cousins who never got to meet their grandparents and a few more that were too young to remember a lot about them. They will go their whole lives without ever meeting or knowing much about their grandparents.

The memories I have of my grandparents are something I never want to lose. I remember playing dress-up at Grandma's house and throwing a ball up and down the laundry chute. I remember skating in the basement and playing cars on the kitchen floor. I also recall all the Fourth of July celebrations I spent at the lake with Grandma and going for long walks with her at dusk. I remember visiting my other grandma and her always having some kind of present for me. Although I was very young I can remember sitting on my grandpa's lap and him asking me for hugs. I also have clear memories of the drives to Wyoming to see my other grandpa and playing Frisbee in the back yard. Each of my grandparents had their own distinct smell. It was a good smell, the smell that grandparents have. It was their smell and only their smell. The memories of all the good times are things I can share with my little cousins, but the smell is something they will never know. It cannot be described.

I also have memories of not such good times. I have an extremely vivid memory of each of their funerals. I describe the weather that day, the somber mood, the way the church looked. I can also see their faces the last time I saw them, right before the casket was closed. I remember the day my grandma died after her fight with lung cancer. She didn't want to stay in the hospital so she was staying with my aunt and uncle and cousins. I was sitting on the front porch steps with my cousin when my mom and aunt called us in to tell us. I remember going up to her room and seeing her. Her eyes and mouth were closed and her chest not moving. She looked peaceful, but I would not touch her. I was eight at the time and I guess I was frightened, but if I could do it over again, I would hold her hand and give her a kiss goodbye. I can also recollect the night my dad got a call from one of his mom's friends saying she had not been answering her phone. My dad went to her house to check on her and she had passed away. I remember when he called to tell us he had found her.

There are too many people in the world that don't take the time to just enjoy life or enjoy the time they have with loved ones. There are so many sayings about "living life to the fullest," " live each day as if it's your last," or "there's no time like the present." I believe that there is truth in all these sayings. I believe when given the opportunities, they should be taken. You never know when or if you will get the chance again. I also think if there is something that you want to say to someone, you should say it and not put it off. Death can come so suddenly. There are thousands of people that die each day, from newborns to centenarians.

Life itself is my most important *law of life*. Death touches everyone, whether it is very personal or a national death, it touches everyone's heart. I ask you to think about how important your life is to you and what your life means to others. Also think about all the loved ones in your life. If they passed away, would there be something you wish you had said or done? A life is something that can never be relived. You only have one chance at it.

Lisa plans to attend college and would like to have a career working with children. She shares, "I hope my essay touches people and makes them think about what is truly important in life."

◦—

OMAHA *LAWS OF LIFE* ESSAY CONTEST

When Carolin Whitaker met Sir John Templeton in 1999, one of the topics they discussed was the essay contest. Several months later Ms. Whitaker, an investment advisor, was with a group of her clients, and she told them about the contest. Everyone looked at each other and said: "We can do this in Omaha!"

Ms. Whitaker next met with Tracy Wernsman, Head of the English Area for Omaha Public Schools. Since their first meeting, Ms. Wernsman has been an indefatigable champion of the contest. During the pilot year, the contest was held at Northwest and South High Schools. Many of Ms. Whitaker's clients served as judges, and an attractive booklet of the winning essays was printed and distributed throughout Omaha. Next year, Ms. Whitaker and the Omaha Public Schools plan to expand the contest to eight area high schools.

Individual contributors to the contest include Rob and Tamra Bengston, Connie Boeka, Sherri Coffelt, Don and Jeanette Corley, Mary Fosmer, June George, Jack and Fran Keown, Dr. Arden Larsen, Joanne Loers, David Peterson, JoAnne Schafer, Barb Shellhammer, Sarah Voss, and Mike and Carolin Whitaker. Two local businesses, Family Dental Center and First Data Resources, also support the contest.

"I am very optimistic about the future of our country and world," explains Carolin Whitaker. "I am also optimistic about the moral strength and character of our young people. The essay contest allows their moral strength and character to shine through!" ✳

Indexes

CONTEST LOCATIONS

United States

CONTEST SPONSORS

INDIVIDUALS
WITH CONTEST LOCATIONS

Ellis and Jane Jones,
Mankato, Minnesota, 164

Leroy and Anita Jordan,
Mankato, Minnesota, 164

Lynn Joseph,
Southern California, 137

Mike Joseph
Southern California, 136

Jack and Fran Keown,
Omaha, Nebraska, 177

Don Kvasnicka,
Mankato, Minnesota, 164

Arden Larsen, *Omaha, Nebraska,* 177

Joanne Loers,
Omaha, Nebraska, 177

David Peterson, *Omaha, Nebraska,* 177

Warren A. Romaine, Jr., *Montgomery County, North Carolina*, 20, 169

Mr. and Mrs. S.B. "Skeet" Rymer,
Bradley County, Tennessee, 13

JoAnne Schafer, *Omaha, Nebraska,* 177

Carl and Rita Schoenstedt,
Mankato, Minnesota, 164

Barb Shellhammer,
Omaha, Nebraska, 177

Bren Simon,
Palm Beach County, Florida, 33

Mr. and Mrs. Staut, *Fairbanks, Alaska*, 115

Sir John Templeton, *Franklin County, Tennessee*, 3, 5

Dr. John M. Templeton, Jr.,
Newtown Square, Pennsylvania, 51–52

Dr. Pina Templeton, *Newton Square, Pennsylvania and Philadelphia, Pennsylvania*, 51–52, 74, 82

Sara Voss, *Omaha, Nebraska,* 177

Willard and Pat Walker,
Point Lookout, Missouri, 134

Mike and Carolin Whitaker,
Omaha, Nebraska, 177

Frederic "Fritz" Wolfe, *Hickory, North Carolina*, 29, 77

FOUNDATIONS

John and Shirley Davies Foundation,
Cincinnati, Ohio, 99

H&H Foundation, *Lima, Ohio*, 29

Joseph Family Foundation,
Southern California, 135–136, 138, 140–141, 143–147

MetLife Foundation, *State of Florida*, 79

Quantum Foundation, *Palm Beach County, Florida*, 33

Soli Deo Gloria Foundation,
State of Mississippi, 22

Wayzata Community Foundation,
Wayzata, Minnesota, 42, 44

Wilcox Foundation,
Southern California and Shreveport, Louisiana, 136, 161

Zimmerman Foundation, *State of Wyoming*, 62

BUSINESSES

Ad Color, *Guilford County, North Carolina*, 169

Alvin Bowling Center, *Alvin, Texas*, 46

Alvin Golf & Country Club,
Alvin, Texas, 46

Anchor Bank, *Wayzata, Minnesota*, 44

Austin Auto Repair, Inc.,
Mankato, Minnesota, 164

Bailey School Supplies,
State of Wyoming, 62

Burger King of Mankato, *Mankato, Minnesota*, 164

Carolina Bank, *Guilford County, North Carolina*, 169

Central Carolina Bank, *Guilford County, North Carolina*, 169

Super Warehouse Foods, *Alvin, Texas*, 46

Taylor Credit Union, *Medford, Wisconsin*, 121

Time Federal Savings Bank, *Medford, Wisconsin*, 121

US Bancorp Piper Jaffray, *Mankato, Minnesota*, 164

VF Corporation, *Guilford County, North Carolina*, 169

Wells Fargo Bank, *Mankatao, Minnesota*, 164

Whataburger Restaurant, *Alvin, Texas*, 46

Z-99 Radio, *Mankato, Minnesota*, 164

COMMUNITY ORGANIZATIONS

Alvin Community Center, *Alvin, Texas*, 46

Bayou Wildlife Park, *Alvin, Texas*, 46

Carlyle Junior High School Yearbook, *Carlyle, Illinois*, 101

Center for Youth Issues, *multiple locations*, 91, 94, 96, 101, 124, 152, 155, 169

Character Counts! Mid-Shore Community, *Talbot County, Maryland*, 129

CHARACTER*plus*, *St. Louis, Missouri*, 165–166

Chena Kiwanis Club, *Fairbanks, Alaska*, 115

Christian Education Movement, *United Kingdom*, 41

Clayton Rotary Club, *Clayton, Missouri*, 85, 87

Dakota Meadows PTO, *Mankato, Minnesota*, 164

East High School PTO, *Mankato, Minnesota*, 164

Easton Rotary Youth and Community Fund, *Talbot County, Maryland*, 129

Fairbanks Lions Club, *Fairbanks, Alaska*, 115

Florida Education Fund, *State of Florida*, 78–79

Greensboro Merchants Association, *Guilford County, North Carolina*, 169

Guilford County Character Education Council, *Guilford County, North Carolina*, 169

Hickory Jaycees, *Hickory, North Carolina*, 77

Immanuel Lutheran School PTO, *Mankato, Minnesota*, 164

International Education and Resource Network, *Worldwide*, 102-112

Jesse Helms Center, *State of North Carolina*, 65

Junior Achievement Russia, *Russian Federation*, 117

Junto Club, *Winona, Minnesota*, 38

Kiwanis Club of Fairbanks, *Fairbanks, Alaska*, 115

The Learning Partnership, *Ontario, Canada*, 149, 150

Livingston Parish School Board, *Livingston Parish, Louisiana*, 124

Mankato Sertoma, *Mankato, Minnesota*, 164

Medford Kiwanis, *Medford, Wisconsin*, 119, 121

Mississippi High School Activities Association, *State of Mississippi*, 22

Napa County Board of Supervisors, *Napa County, California*, 126

Napa County Commission on Self-Esteem, *Napa County, California*, 125, 126

City of Naples, *Collier County, Florida*, 48

Northwestern School District, *Albion, Pennsylvania*, 152

Optimist Club of Georgetown,
Georgetown, Ontario, Canada, 88–89

Palm Beach Roundtable, *Palm Beach County, Florida*, 33

Peer Helpers, *Carlyle, Illinois*, 101

Peer Mediation Group, *Mayfield, Ohio*, 94

Presbyterian Church,
Mankato, Minnesota, 164

School District of Clayton, *Clayton, Missouri*, 87

Soroptomists of Fairbanks,
Fairbanks, Alaska, 115

Spirit Lake Noon Kiwanis Club,
Dickinson County, Iowa, 69

Spirit Lake Sunrise Kiwanis Club,
Dickinson County, Iowa, 69

Teen Institute,
Mayfield, Ohio, 94

Theta Alpha,
Bryn Athyn, Pennsylvania, 55

Winona Golden K Kiwanis Club,
Winona, Minnesota, 38

YMCA of Greater New York,
New York, New York, 24, 26

YPO 49'ers,
Collier County, Florida, 48

Colleges and Universities

Alvin Community College,
Alvin, Texas, 46

Bryan College, *Rhea County, Tennessee*, 155

Casper College, *State of Wyoming*, 61

Centenary College of Louisiana,
Shreveport, Louisiana, 161

College of the Ozarks, *Point Lookout, Missouri*, 130, 134

Florida State University, *Leon County, Florida*, 70–71

Greensboro College, *Guilford County, North Carolina*, 169–170

Northwood University, *Palm Beach County, Florida*, 33–34

St. Mary's University of Minnesota,
Winona, Minnesota, 38

ESSAY THEMES

POSITIVE CHARACTER TRAITS

PRINCIPLES FOR SUCCESSFUL LIVING

Sir John Templeton

S IR JOHN TEMPLETON graduated from Yale University and was a Rhodes Scholar at Balliol College, Oxford University. He is universally regarded as a pioneer in the development of high-yield globally diversified mutual funds, founding the highly successful Templeton Growth Fund and Templeton World Fund. His creativity and wisdom as an investor brought the benefits of top-flight counsel to ordinary people and helped create the reality of a "people's capitalism."

Born in rural Winchester, Tennessee, John Templeton once dreamed of a career in full-time religious service. His first major philanthropic endeavor was in 1972 with the establishment of the Templeton Prize for Progress in Religion. Today the Templeton Prize is the world's largest monetary award at roughly $1.3 million. The first Prize was given to the late Mother Teresa of Calcutta. Since then the Templeton Prize has been awarded each year, and recognizes a living individual who has shown extraordinary originality in advancing humanity's understanding of God and/or spirituality. Other past recipients have included Reverend Billy Graham, author Aleksandr Solzhenitsyn, and theoretical physicist and author Freeman J. Dyson.

In 1987, John Templeton was knighted by Queen Elizabeth II for his philanthropic efforts, which included his endowment of Templeton College, Oxford. After selling the Templeton Group of mutual funds in 1992, he focused his talents on pioneering new ways to create value and stimulate progress through philanthropy. Since then, he has authored and edited over a dozen books. One of his most recent, *Worldwide Laws of Life*, is a collection of 200 eternal spiritual principles drawn from the works of philosophers ranging from Socrates to Benjamin Franklin.

Established in 1987, the John Templeton Foundation supports hundreds of programs worldwide, which serve three chief purposes. The first is to stimulate serious, rigorous, progress-generating links between the sciences and all religions. The second purpose is to encourage character development in schools and colleges. The third purpose is to stimulate greater appreciation worldwide for the benefits of freedom and free competition.